GREAT myths *of* Business

Other Books by William Davis

Three Years' Hard Labour
Merger Mania
Money Talks
Have Expenses, Will Travel
It's No Sin to be Rich
Money in the 1980s
The Rich: A Study of the Species
Fantasy: A Practical Guide to Escapism
The Corporate Infighter's Handbook
The Super Salesman's Handbook
The Innovators
Children of the Rich
The Lucky Generation: A Positive View of the 21st Century

GREAT myths *of* Business

EVERYTHING YOU THINK
YOU KNOW IS WRONG

William Davis

KOGAN
PAGE

This publication is designed to provide accurate and authoritative information in regard to the subject matter covered. It is sold with the understanding that the publisher is not engaged in rendering legal, accounting, or other professional service. If legal advice or other expert assistance is required, the services of a competent professional person should be sought.

Inquiries concerning reproduction outside those terms should be sent to the publishers at the undermentioned address:

Kogan Page Limited
163 Central Ave., Suite 4
Hopkins Professional Building
Dover, New Hampshire 03820

ISBN: 0-7494-2253X

Printed in the United States of America
98 99 00 10 9 8 7 6 5 4 3 2 1

Contents

Preface

A PREFACE SHOULD EXPLAIN WHY THE BOOK has been written. The short answer is that, after more than 40 years of close involvement in the business world, I felt the urge to expose the difference between myth and reality.

As a financial editor of leading British newspapers I helped to perpetuate some of the myths. My excuse is that I read too many management books and self-serving press releases, interviewed too many tycoons who did not always tell the truth, and wrote too many articles because they made a good story. You may feel that this book amounts to a lengthy confession by a repentant sinner, and you would probably be right.

My eyes were opened when I went into business myself, late in the 1970s. Until then, I had been an observer. I had a ringside seat but I was not actually inside those ropes, slugging it out with skillful and determined opponents. I thought I knew it all, but I was wrong. You never know the difference between myth and reality until you have put your savings, reputation and emotions on the line in the sport called business.

I use the word "sport" deliberately because it is just that for many ambitious people. Making money is important, of course, but it is by no means the only motive. For some, to be sure, the driving force is greed and nothing else. But once you have made a few millions all kinds of other factors tend to come into play — love of power, the desire to build a business empire which you can leave to your children, or simply the urge to prove that you are smarter than everyone else. Many tycoons create their own myths and end up believing in them. So they push ahead, even though they have already made more money than they can ever hope to spend. They have, or pretend to have, an unshakable faith in their own genius.

I can honestly say that I have never fallen into that category. I am rich, through my own efforts, but I know my limitations. I could never be a Rupert Murdoch, much as the idea may appeal to me. I have learned, however, what it is like to take risks, to confront daunting challenges, to taste both victory and defeat. This books seeks to share some of the lessons I have learned in the process.

My home is in London but I have also spent a great deal of time in the United States, where I still have close business links. I have written for publications like *The New York Times* and *Time* magazine, and have talked to many friends who are at the sharp end of American business life. I have tried to bring an international perspective to the task, which I hope you will find useful. If business has become "global" it is surely appropriate to share experiences and views.

I am indebted to my publishers for giving me the opportunity to express controversial opinions, and to Karen Huxley for her editorial assistance.

I should also explain why you will find the words "he" and "business-men" throughout this book. No slight is intended; as you will see, I am well aware of the increasingly important role of women in business. It simply seemed to me clumsy to keep saying "he or she." I hope I will be forgiven.

The 21st century will provide many exciting opportunities as well as new challenges. I am an incurable optimist, so I look forward to them despite the fact that I am now 64. I am convinced that young people, including my own children and grandchildren, have an exciting future. I am all in favor of dreams and ambitions, but it clearly helps to understand the realities of business life. This book is dedicated to them.

Popular Myths

"MYTHOLOGY," THE LATE PRESIDENT KENNEDY once said, "distracts us everywhere — in government as in business, in politics as in economics, in foreign affairs as in domestic policy." He was right, but politicians must take at least part of the blame. They, along with the media and alleged experts, have created and nurtured many enduring myths.

People like to believe that there is an answer to everything, and their interpretation of events around them tends to be influenced by their beliefs. The belief does not necessarily have to be true; some fragment of truth will do. The motive leading to the propagation of a myth is not the scientific search for it; it is a subconscious desire for explanations. The test of an explanation is often in its effectiveness in advancing some special cause rather than its veracity as determined by objective appraisal. This is why old myths tend to have long lives and new ones are constantly created.

Politicians have always encouraged the widespread belief that they are "running the country." At its most absurd level this has led to the myth that one individual — a President or Prime Minister — makes all the decisions. In reality, governments have much less power than they like to pretend. In the public sector, numerous decisions are made by bureaucrats. Elected officials are expected to accept responsibility for them, but they cannot possibly deal with all the details on their own. In

1

the private sector, business leaders make the running. Even they, however, leave a great deal to their managers, especially in large and complex organizations.

The media tends to ignore or underplay this because it suits journalists to focus on personalities. But most of us know that human progress does not come from politicians and tycoons alone; it comes from scientists, engineers, artists, entrepreneurs and other human beings acting individually or in combination. The purpose of government, in a free society, is to provide a framework in which individual citizens and voluntary associations can follow their self-chosen purposes. There must be limits, but the State cannot and should not attempt to assume total control. Even in Russia, this simple fact is nowadays widely accepted. Karl Marx created many myths about capitalism and the alleged merits of communism. People believed him because they wanted to believe that there had to be a better way. We all know what happened.

Marx was wrong on so many counts that it's hard to know where to start. Capitalism did not collapse; on the contrary, it is now embraced by countries within the former Soviet Union. Material misery has not increased inside the capitalist world; in most industrial nations, the working classes have seen a substantial improvement in their economic conditions. Agriculture has not become subject to concentrated industrial ownership; attempts to achieve that aim in the Soviet bloc were a dismal failure. The middle class has not vanished; it has grown tremendously. Independent businessmen and self-employed people vastly outnumber big capitalists. It is important to remember all this because a new generation could so easily fall for the same kind of nonsense.

Economics is especially plagued with myths because this is a field in which everyone considers himself to be an expert. Many people refuse to discard their beliefs, even when they are shown to be wrong or out of date, because they think that their economic sense is better than anyone else's. They get angry when their deeply-held convictions are described as myths. But it is necessary to identify erroneous ideas so that valid ones can take their place. The task is not helped by the fact that economics is beset with jargon. It can, and does, lead to misunderstanding and the formation of beliefs which might be more readily challenged if the lay-man knew what economists are talking about. I shall return to this sub-ject in this book, but let us consider some of the more common myths.

If Someone Gains, Someone Else Loses

It is widely assumed that people who make money must be doing so at the expense of others. This may be true of the stock market, or horse racing, or a poker game, but it is certainly not true of most everyday business transactions. If I buy a new suit, or a car, or a bag of groceries, it is a voluntary act which I enter into in the full knowledge that the retailer expects to make a profit. I don't mind, because I want those things and I am willing to pay for them. In short, I receive an item which is of greater value to me than the item with which I parted. We may argue about the price, but both of us gain something by the exchange.

Unfortunately, the myth is often extended to cover whole groups. If one country trades with another, and visibly improves its position by doing so, the myth holds that the improvement must have come at the expense of the other country. But the second country is also likely to have bene-fited from the exchange — it may, for example, have sold raw materials or locally-produced goods and earned much-needed foreign exchange or stimulated employment.

The myth that all wealth is accumulated by exploitation can lead to demands for government intervention and other undesirable attempts to prevent us from doing what we, as individuals, think is in our best inter-est. In times of recession, there are invariably calls for local industry to be protected from foreign competition. The assumption is that trade can be a one-way street, with the country selling abroad buying only home-produced goods. You don't have to be an economist to see the flaws in that argument. If we refuse to buy from them, they can do the same to us. Coddling of local industries will almost certainly raise the cost of liv-ing. Protectionist policies have done a lot of harm in the past and would do so again. It is not a realistic option — in modern economies.

To Reward People Equally is to Treat Them Fairly

This is the old socialist myth, perpetuated by people who believe in enforced equality. It didn't work in the Soviet Union, and it doesn't work in a free society. Yet it still turns up in the programs of left-wing organizations, who seem determined to reduce everyone to the lowest common denominator. To demand equal rewards is simply to demand a regimented society.

The Soviets claimed to believe in the principle, but, just as in George Orwell's *Animal Farm*, some were "more equal than others." The bureaucratic élite arranged things in such a way that the leaders always came out on top. The rest were supposed to settle for what the state regarded as equality, but it did not mean that they were treated fairly.

It was entirely reasonable to expect that, for example, doctors and scientists should be properly rewarded for years of study and special skills. It would have been fair. But they were not, which eventually proved to be one of the main reasons why the whole rotten edifice collapsed. What matters is equality of opportunity, which is an altogether different concept.

Marxists believe in another dictum: "to each according to his needs." The trouble with that, of course, is that the bureaucracy assumes the right to judge those needs. It has nothing to do with fairness; it has everything to do with the obsessive urge to decide how others should live.

Wages Can be Increased Substantially Without Affecting Prices or Employment

Labor unions have always loved this one; it plays well with the rank and file. They see a company making big profits and demand a larger share. But labor is not immune to economic laws. If costs go up, something has to give. Companies need profits, not only to pay dividends to their shareholders but also to make investments in new plant and equipment. Their main yardstick is return on capital employed. They will try to pass on cost increases, in the form of higher prices, but if that is difficult because of competitive pressures, they will reduce the workforce. Modern technology has made it easier to do so than ever before. Most trade union leaders understand this perfectly well, but reckon that they are more likely to keep their own jobs if they go along with the myth.

The Government Has to Pay Its Debts, Just as You and I Do

Politicians often say this in response to constant demands for more public spending. But it is a myth. The government can create money to pay its bills and run a deficit every year for as long as it likes. There are strong arguments against the practice: at some point it is inflationary. But it can be done — and is.

This myth says that there is some maximum level that debt can safely reach; if this level is exceeded, the country will be plunged into bankruptcy. Not so. The national debt has been around ever since the beginning of the nation. It is far larger now than earlier generations would have considered "safe," but America has not gone bust.

The total amount the government owes — the accumulation of all the past deficits — is now roughly $5 trillion, including funds invested in U.S. Treasury securities. The debt that is held by the public, including foreigners, is about $3.8 trillion. When the government spends less or collects more in revenues, the deficit is reduced. If the deficit is smaller, the national debt grows more slowly. To reduce the national debt, the deficit must be turned into a surplus. The last time this happened was about 30 years ago. But not all deficits are bad. If the economy is slipping into recession, the deficit represents a government stimulus to the economy that can help to end the recession.

There is an important difference between debt that is held internally and that which is owed to another country. In the latter case, we must earn foreign currency so that we can make payment. But the popular idea that the "trade gap" must be closed if we want to survive is another myth. Countries like the United States get a large part of their foreign exchange earnings from so-called "invisibles" — money earned from

financial services, transport, tourism, dividends paid on overseas investments, and so on. This substantial contribution to the balance of payments helps to make up for any deficit that may arise from trading in
manufactured goods.

State-Owned Industries Belong to the People

Only in theory. In practice we have no claim on them of any kind.
Indeed, we may lose by the arrangement if they have monopoly powers
(which allow them to fix whatever prices they like) or if they have to be
subsidized through higher taxes.

The British Labor party used to be strongly in favor of nationalization.
It argued that governments must control 'the commanding heights' of
the economy in order to safeguard public services. This is still the view
taken by the Left, but the present leadership is less enthusiastic. The
credit must go to Margaret Thatcher who, as Prime Minister, privatized
most industries formerly owned by the state.

British Steel used to be one of the lamest ducks in the public sector.
Today it is the world's most profitable steelmaker. British Airways, too,
was a disaster until it was privatized. Other countries have followed
Britain's lead. The people now have much more direct ownership
because they or their pension funds have shares in the industries. They
have benefited in other ways: prices of gas, telecommunications and
electricity have all dropped substantially in real terms. We still love to
complain about the services we get, but it would be churlish not to
acknowledge that there has been a major improvement in many areas.

The World is Running Out of Oil and Raw Materials

This, too, is a myth. Remember the "oil crisis" of the early 1970s? It was
close to a panic. Motorists were shocked to find that they could no
longer fill up where and when they wanted, and within days the media
began to make all kinds of gloomy predictions. The world, it seemed,
was running out of the black stuff which had kept cars on the road,
planes in the air, ships on the seas. We would have to walk, freeze, sit in

the dark. Good-bye to the Mercedes, the jet, baths, central heating, neon lights, taxis and trains. An era had ended.

But, of course, it hadn't. The crisis was phony — a concerted effort by producers to put up prices. The world was not running out of oil. The fears were baseless.

During the 1980s there was talk of another oil crisis. This time, though, it meant that we had too much of the stuff. It was a crisis for oil producers, not for the likes of us.

Estimates of reserves at any moment of time never represent true reserves in the sense of being all that can ever be found. They are the reserves which have been worth finding, given the price, prospect of demand, and cost of exploration. Each decade has seen the discovery of new sources and the development of more advanced techniques of extraction.

More than a hundred years ago, the British economist William Stanley Jevons predicted an inevitable shortage of coal within a short period of time. But although demand for coal has since been far greater than anticipated, known coal reserves are estimated to be enough to last for another 600 years. Reserves of oil should last for at least another century. Meanwhile, other sources of energy (especially nuclear power) are making a significant impact.

In countries like America the demand for raw materials is likely to decline in the 21st century because of a variety of factors, notably the more efficient use of resources, an increased emphasis on services rather than on the old smokestack industries, new technology, and the development of alternatives.

A variation of the doomsday theory is that the world will soon be unable to feed its growing population. This is a myth which made its debut as long ago as 1798, when Thomas Malthus warned that we faced death from starvation. His *Essay on the Principle of Population* had a profound influence on social and economic thinking. The principle was simple: unchecked breeding of man causes the population to grow by geometrical progression, whereas the food supply cannot grow so rapidly. The remedy, he thought, was prudence and self-restraint, which society should reinforce by refusing charity or public support for any families which could not support themselves. In other words, let them die. It was a harsh prescription for a man of God to advocate (Malthus was a clergyman who had three children of his own), but he maintained that it was the only humanitarian solution in its ultimate effect, short-sighted benevolence being a palliative which could only make the situation worse.

Britain's ruling class of the day was so frightened by the Malthusian doctrine that it adopted policies which today's generation would find outrageous. They were certainly unnecessary. His prediction proved to be wide of the mark. The supply of food in Britain more than kept pace with a leaping population due to factors he did not foresee, notably a significant increase in farming output. This later became known as the Agricultural Revolution but it consisted of piecemeal improvements — rotation of crops, new breeding techniques, better estate management, enclosure of common lands and draining of wetlands, new agricultural implements, and so on. Britain also embarked on its Industrial Revolution, which led to a sharp increase in productivity and national wealth. The country could well afford to import whatever food it could not grow at home.

It would plainly be foolish not to acknowledge that the rise in the world's population is cause for concern — or, for that matter, that many people suffer from malnutrition. But the rate of growth has dropped in recent years and it is generally expected that at some point the population will stabilize. In developed countries, it may actually go into reverse. Meantime, the world is not running out of food. Contemporary famines and shortages in some parts are mainly due to wars, natural disasters, and the inadequate distribution of food. Economists reckon that billions more people could be fed by bringing more land under cultivation and introducing further improvements in growing techniques. Farms should become even more productive as advances in genetic engineering improve the yield of plants and animals. The aquaculture business is also set for rapid expansion; we will, increasingly, raise and harvest fish instead of hunting them.

You may feel that all this sounds too complacent. Perhaps it does. I have no wish to be portrayed as a Pollyanna, but what happened two centuries ago showed the danger of spreading false alarms. There is certainly no reason to fear that countries like Britain and the United States will run short of food in the years ahead.

Banks Are as Safe as Houses

This is one of the more beneficial myths. The basis of any financial system is confidence: if it dwindles, as it did during the Great Depression, the whole structure can collapse like a house of cards. It is, therefore, essential to maintain some beliefs. Much effort has gone into building safeguards against doubts. A run on the banking system would have dreadful consequences, which is why no government could stay on the sidelines if a major clearing bank got into serious trouble. Most people know it, and it underpins public confidence. But the same does not necessarily apply to smaller banks. The government of the day may well decide (as it did in the case of Barings) that the threat is not great enough to warrant financial intervention.

"Safe as houses" is, in any case, a cliché which does not stand up to closer examination, if one takes it to mean that you cannot go wrong by investing in property. Numerous people have lost money by buying into houses at the wrong price, at the wrong time, and in the wrong location.

Business Needs a Strong Dollar

This is known as the macho theory of currency. Many people see their nation's currency as some kind of virility symbol, and a strong dollar is a source of pride. But the idea that it helps business to compete in world markets is a myth. The opposite tends to happen, because it makes

American products more expensive and imports cheaper. Tourism, a major industry, is also affected because foreign visitors find that their own currency doesn't buy as much as it did before.

A country's exchange rate is a price — nothing more. Many governments have found that devaluation can give a big boost to exports, which helps to create more jobs.

An intriguing question, as we head into the 21st century, is what will happen to the dollar when the planned single European currency appears on the scene. The euro will be its first real competitor since it supplanted sterling as the world's dominant currency. Some economists estimate that more than $1 trillion may shift from dollars to euro.

The aim is to fix national exchange rates in January 1999 and to have a transitional period until 2002, after which the euro alone will be legal tender. A lot of things could go wrong in between. It is possible that the initial effect will be to boost the dollar, rather than to weaken it, but it is also possible that the euro will be strong right from the start. The new European Central Bank will take a tough line on inflation.It should mean rising interest rates, which would attract investors to fixed-income assets in euros.

My guess is that the dollar will probably remain the leading currency indefinitely, but that the creation of the euro will narrow, and perhaps eventually close, the present monetary gap between the United States and Europe.

The Myth that Gurus Have All the Answers

ONE OF THE GREAT BUSINESS MYTHS OF THE 1990s is that management theorists have all the answers. It might be easier to believe if more of them had actually run a business and if they did not contradict each other with such maddening regularity.

The doyen of the tribe, Peter Drucker, says he hates the word "guru," thinking it synonymous with "charlatan." He candidly admits that he has never been part of an organization. He has never run a business, never met a payroll, never worried as a manager. He says he wouldn't be any good at it. "We know nothing about motivation," he once told a business school audience. "All we can do is write books about it."

Unlike so many of his fellow theorists, Drucker is being unduly modest. He has taught new ways of thinking about management and the organization, and he is widely credited with inventing privatization — though it was Margaret Thatcher who put it into practice. Drucker has always made a point of being provocative, and there is no doubt that he has a considerable influence on the world of business. He pioneered the now well-known concept of "management by objectives," which shifts the focus from process to goals, to the purpose of the activity rather than the activity itself. Instead of asking "What do I do?," the manager is led to ask: "What is the objective towards which we are working?" Organizational objectives, he taught, must grow out of a thorough knowledge of what the business is and what it should be. Specific targets, not abstractions, render it possible to make specific assignments. Objectives should enable management to do five things: organize and explain the whole range of business phenomena in a few general statements; test these statements; predict behavior; gauge the soundness of decisions before they are made; and to analyze and improve performance. The structure of a firm, he argued, should follow its strategy. "Organization is not an end in itself, but a means to an end of business performance and business results."

The argument makes obvious sense, which probably explains why many academics have always looked down on him. In their eyes he commits the ultimate sin: he simplifies. Here is Drucker, talking about his approach to consulting:

> The contribution I make to a client is basically to be very stupid and very dense; ask simple, fundamental questions; demand that he be thoughtful with the answers; and demand that he makes decisions on what is important. I feel very strongly that a client who leaves my office feeling that he has learned a lot that he didn't know before is a stupid client; either that, or I haven't done my job. He should leave the office saying: "I know all this — but why haven't I done anything about it?"

Judging by their books and lectures, other gurus clearly feel that this won't do. They have a passion for convoluted theories and fancy jargon accompanied by incomprehensible diagrams. It often turns out to be pretentious waffle, but it impresses the people who pay the bills.

Guru-Speak

The guru industry has prospered because managers are afraid of change and not sure how to handle it. They look to gurus for solutions. Some also think it will help their careers if they are seen to be in touch with the latest thinking. I have attended many meetings at which managers spouted fashionable buzzwords without being able to explain what they meant. The usual response of their colleagues has been to let it pass (no one wants to display ignorance) or nod in confirmation, which they hope will be taken to mean that they, too, are up-to-date.

I once saw a splendid cartoon by Leo Cullum. A guy is coming through the front door to be greeted by his wife; he's looking disheveled, exhausted, and shocked. "They changed all the buzzwords," he explains, "but they didn't tell me."

You can easily make up your own jargon. The basic name of the game is never to use a simple word or phrase if you can find a complex one. A garden, for example, should always be called "a recreational eco-unit," which makes a spade a "manually-operated recreational eco-unit maintenance tool." Once you have mastered the art, you should be able to stun the meeting into awed silence. Throw in, for good measure, a qualifying "of course" — as in "of course if the systematized multiphase imputation conflicts with the subordinated motivational framework, it may be advisable to utilize the restructured tactical procedure." It takes courage to challenge that kind of statement.

Getting it Wrong

Much has been said and written about two of the most recent fads, downsizing and re-engineering. Both these ugly words have been widely used as euphemisms for a much older practice — giving people the sack. The guru who made downsizing fashionable, Wall Street economist Stephen Roach, has since recanted. Others have also conceded that making companies thinner does not necessarily make them fitter. After so many years of relentless cost-cutting it may seem like a breathtaking reversal of thinking, but we should not be surprised. In modern management theory, such changes of heart are the rule rather than the exception.

Re-engineering is an attempt to break an organization down into its component parts and then put some of them back together again. Managers have been told that they need to tear up their old blueprints and start with a clean sheet of paper if they want to survive. The argument is not without merit — some companies have made it work — but is another idea which has probably passed its sell-by date. The obsession with process (which Drucker warned against) has tended to make senior management neglect what really matters — having the right products or services and ensuring customer satisfaction.

Many gurus do not appear to be in the slightest bit embarrassed when things do not turn out as they said they would. Tom Peters, one of the best-known members of the tribe, was the co-author of a best-selling book published in 1982, *In Search of Excellence*. It sought to identify outstanding American companies and the secrets of their success. Nothing wrong with that, but two-thirds of them subsequently fell from grace. Peters blithely declared in his next volume that there were no "excellent" companies. It was by no means the first time that he had contradicted himself, but he continues to have a loyal following. His disciples would no doubt argue that there can be no certainties in a rapidly changing world. They would be right, but surely this suggests that one should not take everything the gurus say at face value.

Like others, Peters seems fanatic about change. In *Thriving on Chaos*, he warned the heads of companies that "if you are not reorganizing, pretty substantially, every six to 12 months you are probably out of touch with the times." The obvious response is that such constant turmoil is likely to be counterproductive. People like him do not have to deal with the consequences.

I am a great believer in the merits of change but the idea that it always leads to better things is a myth. The late Patrick Hutber, who was city editor of the *Sunday Telegraph*, invented a law which is still much-quoted: "improvement means deterioration." We have all seen examples of that. London's Heathrow airport has been "improved" but the main result is that it has been turned into a vast shopping complex, which forces passengers to walk greater distances to their planes. Some things should not change: if you have a highly successful product, brand name, or service, it would plainly be foolish to discard it for the sake of novelty.

As many companies have found, the process of change is frequently difficult and tortuous. One of the dangers to be avoided is plunging in too deeply and adopting a system or philosophy that has not been fully tested. Many change programs have been delayed for a considerable time by equipment that would not perform to the expected standard. Expensive development work and modifications have to take place which are disruptive to the organization. The workforce may put up resistance, because the list of changes appears endless and affects the beliefs and practices that are fundamental for many trade union officials. If it involves job losses, as it so frequently does, there may be strikes and other problems. Sometimes the managers who are leading the way are dismissed because the program has run into difficulties or failed to produce the stated benefits on time. They may be replaced by new leaders with different beliefs who will overturn the previous ideas.

None of this means that change should not happen — in many cases, it may be inevitable. But the people who make it must not get too carried away with visions and idealism. They are part of the process, but they must be tempered by commercial business realities.

All organizations are undergoing a degree of change all the time as part of normal management. The real challenge comes when significant initiatives are planned that could radically alter the way the organization operates. There is much to be said for introducing them in phases and adopting tried and tested ideas and technology rather than experimenting with something that has yet to prove its value.

The guru industry tends to concentrate on big companies because they have the most problems (or think they have) and because that's where the money is. It has also had a considerable influence in the public sector, which is under continuous pressure to increase efficiency through reorganization. Politicians are anxious to show that they can do "more with less," particularly in areas like health care and education, and will look at anything which appears to hold out the opportunity to manage things better. In America, Vice President Al Gore has said that agencies will have to "justify why they should continue to exist at all." In Britain, many people take a similar view. Civil servants are understandably reluctant to relinquish control (they want to keep their own jobs) and some are quietly resisting change. They pay lip-service to it, but implementation is something else. Doctors and teachers are more outspoken. They feel that far too much attention is given to management and complain that the endless tinkering with structure and procedure, with its attendant increase in the load of paperwork, is making their tasks more difficult. The best way to make the public sector more efficient, they say, is to fire the managers who get in the way of what really counts.

People who run small companies are even less inclined to pay attention to the theorists. It could be argued that they should make an effort to find out what is going on, because the decisions made by big organizations can affect them — they may result in a loss of business or create new opportunities. But many entrepreneurs reckon that they have no need to read management books or to attend seminars.

Some of the gurus have gripes of their own. They feel that their status is being undermined by the growing numbers of people who seek to get in on their act with self-help books that claim to show how you can "unleash the power within" or to get rich "the easy way." They are particularly annoyed that sports figures and religious groups think they are qualified to give advice on management. In the United States, baseball players have written books on the importance of teamwork and in Britain former rugby captain Will Carling is telling managers how to "apply lessons from the playing field to the workplace." The Maharishi Foundation has set up a school of management which specializes in "training managers to bring unfailing success and continuing progress to their companies" through meditation and levitation.

I can understand their irritation, but there is clearly a demand for this kind of thing and they should not expect to have such a lucrative field all to themselves.

The best theorists stimulate thought and provide genuine insights. It can be of value but, as we have seen, it does not mean that they are necessarily right. The contradictions and frequent revisions are confusing, and many of the theories are of little practical use to most businessmen. I prefer to read books by people like the amiable, iconoclastic Sir John Harvey-Jones, who has based his views on what he learned as head of ICI.

Peter Drucker once said that "before World War II most managers did not know they were managing." It was one of his typical tongue-in-cheek remarks. In fact, the so-called Managerial Revolution began much earlier, when the children and grandchildren of the great industry-builders of the 19th century handed over command of the businesses and capital they had inherited to a new breed of professional managers. Alfred Sloan, who became chairman of General Motors in 1937, invented much of what is still commonplace in business today. When he retired in 1957, General Motors was the largest and in many ways the most successful industrial organization in the world. But the obsession with management theory, which is spreading to Asia and former communist countries in Europe, is a phenomenon of our time.

Gurus attack complacency, and for that they deserve our thanks. But the ultimate responsibility for improvement lies squarely on the shoulders of the audience — whether it is an individual seeking enlightenment in India or a company losing its way in Chicago.

The Consulting Game

Many gurus have followed Drucker into the consulting business, which is a major source of revenue, and less hard work than writing books. They charge fat fees for this advice. Some also run seminars and sell videos, cassettes, and newsletters. The Tom Peters Group in California offers "The Tom Peters Business School in a Box" (I kid you not), which comes complete with 42 "personal agenda cards," 14 "time-cards," and two dice, one colored, one white.

The consulting industry is self-perpetuating and self-proliferating. Gurus keep the momentum going with a constant flow of new ideas, many of which are bunk. Old ones, like strategic planning, have also remained in circulation.

To many of today's businessmen, a management consultant has become almost as essential as a psychiatrist to a Hollywood star. Some use them as a sounding-board for their own ideas, or to justify decisions which have already been taken. (It reassures them that their choice was valid and helps to convince colleagues that what they have decided to do is right.) Some hire consultants so that they have someone else to blame if things don't work out. Many use them as a front for unpleasant tasks, such as downsizing. But they can also provide a fresh perspective and expertise that is lacking in the organization. They often uncover ideas which have been lying around unnoticed or which have been allowed to drift away. Senior managers tend to be more willing to listen to proposals and suggestions from outsiders than to those which come from their own employees. They feel that, because the company has paid for the consultant, that individual should be given careful consideration. It is annoying, but it improves the chances that something will be done.

Inevitably, there are also many businessmen who would not dream of employing a consultant. Their attitude was summed up by Robert Townsend, a former president of Avis, in *Up the Organization*. Management consultants, he said, "waste time, cost money, demoralize and distract your best people, and don't solve problems. They are the people who borrow your watch to tell you what time it is and then walk off with it."

This is an exaggeration, but it contains a sizable element of truth. Consultants are certainly expensive and there is no guarantee that they will produce the hoped-for results. Consultants also tend to create bad vibes among employees, who view them with suspicion because employees don't know what they are there for and what effect their recommendations will have on staff.

Various attempts have been made to define what the game is all about. The most widely accepted definition is, or seems to be, that:

> management consulting is the professional service performed by specially trained and experienced persons in helping managers identify and solve managerial and operating problems of the various institutions in our society; in recommending practical solutions to these problems; and helping to implement them when necessary.

The main trouble with this interpretation is that one cannot be sure about the degree of professionalism one is likely to get. Standards vary considerably. There is no formal education in consulting and you do not need a license to operate. Anyone can call himself a consultant.

Some people go into the business because they have been fired from a management job and cannot get another. It's socially acceptable and can lend you an air of mystery. People are impressed when you tell them that "I'm a management consultant." Some are retired executives who are bored with pruning roses and recognize that there is still a market for their knowledge and experience. Others are ambitious types who reckon that consulting is a good way to the top of a large organization.

Consultants can be classified into three broad categories — individuals or freelancers; small firms, which usually specialize in certain areas; and big, multidisciplinary firms. One of the attractions for entrepreneurial characters is that consulting as a business venture has low overhead and requires little capital as a start-up investment. But they face formidable competition from the major players.

The truth is that much of what consultants do could just as easily be handled by good managers in a large organization. Most assignments are simply a matter of information gathering, data analysis, and a search for common sense solutions. There maybe a strong case for using people with expertise in particular areas, such as marketing and executive search, but business leaders who have to call in generalists for advice are merely advertising their own weakness. Shareholders should draw the obvious conclusion: replace the highly-placed chief executive, perhaps by the consultant.

The management consultant's one big plus, as he never ceases to remind those who employ him, is that he is independent, an unbiased expert who can give advice without fear or favor. Consultants often work on a one-off basis, so they don't have to worry about upsetting anyone. But the independence may be an illusion. Consultants seldom go as far as suggesting that the chief executive should be fired, even if they have concluded that this individual is the main problem. They tend to be equally reluctant to give what in some cases may be the most sensible advice: do nothing. They want more assignments. The ideal state of affairs, for many of them, is to get hooked into a client and never release their grip.

Consultants are generally very good at selling themselves. They have to be, because potential clients have to be persuaded that they need their help. They dress well, project self-confidence, and know how to use all the jargon. They also tend to be good at listening, which flatters the client and gives the consultant the first indication of what may be required of him. The consultant's credibility is, of course, greatly enhanced by working for one of the top firms and having specialist training in a discipline like engineering, accounting, or marketing. Image is important.

A catchphrase which seems to work well is "maximizing economic opportunities." It implies that the company which hires a consulting firm will eventually get something for its money, such as increased profits. But the people who do the selling are not necessarily the ones who do the work. Clients may find that the partner who has made such an impressive pitch will disappear once the agreement has been signed. An "Associate" will take over. That person may be just as good, if not better, but there is often a wide gap between what has been promised and what is actually delivered.

Some consultants have a tendency to borrow the conclusions of one report and adapt it to another. The assumption is that what has worked for company A will also work for company B; in any event, it saves time and effort. The client may, therefore, be paying handsomely for the same report that has already gone to a competitor, which is not supposed to be the purpose of the exercise. The client may also find that important details are being handled by juniors. These consulting associates are often the people who interview employees and customers, prepare charts and graphs, and write the first draft of the report. The client, of course, is charged the full fee.

I am not saying that it is standard procedure — much depends on the reputation of the firm, the size of the fee, and the ability of the client to spot such obvious tactics and, if need be, take appropriate action. But there is no fixed code of ethics.

There must always be someone in management who knows how consultants operate and who can ensure that the company will get something that is truly worthwhile. The biggest mistake one can make is to fall for the myth that, just because they charge so much, all consultants are smart and competent. Some are; some are not.

The best are specialists who are accustomed to tackling specific tasks, or versatile generalists with years of experience who are intellectually honest, resilient, persistent, capable of working alone or as a member of a team, and genuinely willing to put the client's interests first. But every consultant, however competent, can only get results if the client is open-minded, cooperative, and acts on the offered recommendation. Problems must be clearly defined and there must be an agreed set of objectives. The executive should monitor progress and, if the recommendations make sense, insist that management follow through. If the executive fails to do this, no one else is to blame if the whole business turns out to be a waste of time and money.

America's largest telephone company, AT&T, used to be a management consultant's dream. Since the start of the 1990s it has spent more than a billion dollars on consulting. At one time, more than 1,000 firms were crawling all over it. That highly respected journal, *The Economist*, has neatly summed up what happened. The "army of hired thinkers," it says, "encouraged AT&T to make a series of disastrous decisions, including buying NCR, a computer maker, for well above its market value, and announcing huge lay-offs. It also talked the company into adopting some of the silliest management fads around. The plan to revitalize NCR, for example, involved renaming managers 'coaches,' tearing down office doors, and encouraging employees to wear T-shirts bearing the message "putting the moose on the table." But suddenly the party stopped. When AT&T's new boss, John Walter, took over the first thing he did was to kick out the consultants and tell his colleagues to start thinking for themselves."

The Myth of
the Expert MBA

MANAGEMENT CONSULTING COMPANIES LOOK for bright university graduates who will work hard for a modest salary — at least to begin with. The bigger firms will train them before they are let loose on clients, but many others expect them to learn their craft on assignments. The client is, in effect, paying for their further education.

I call it a craft, not a profession, because I don't think that consultants are entitled to bracket themselves with doctors or lawyers. They may have professional qualifications, but the term "management consultant" does not, by itself, deserve the same status.

A university degree is nowadays regarded as a prerequisite, but of course it does not necessarily mean that the graduate has acquired a store of knowledge that is of value in business. The study of history or arts may enrich the mind, and prepare young people for all kinds of occupations, but it does not help them to come to grips with liquidity ratios, restructuring, marketing, salesmanship, and management by objectives.

Universities say that they produce erudite individuals who have demonstrated their ability to learn, think and master difficult subjects. They have a point, but it does not invalidate the argument, put forward by many businessmen, that they should teach more students the practical skills which employers want rather than cram their heads with interesting but unusable facts.

It is an old debate, which will no doubt continue for a long time to come. The number of job-seeking graduates has increased dramatically in recent decades and, as many of them discovered, a degree has lost much of its shine. It helps to explain the popularity of a title which people still find impressive — Master of Business Administration.

The MBA was invented by Harvard University in the 1900s but not imported into Britain until 1965. In the intervening years anyone who wanted it had to study in the United States.

In 1967 several MBAs who had returned to the UK formed the Business Graduates Association, which later became the Association of MBAs — AMBA. They had two aims. The first was to promote formal management education and the merits of the MBA in particular. They also wanted to provide a forum, similar to the alumni associations they had seen in the U.S., for social contact, networking and continued learning through meetings and conferences. It worked so well that a new myth was created: MBAs were the people most likely to succeed in business.

This was never accepted by street-smart entrepreneurs who had left school in their teens to start their own company or who had made their way up the slippery corporate ladder by showing exceptional flair for corporate gamesmanship. Many people, they pointed out, had built great empires without the benefit of a university education, let alone a master's degree in business. The late Soichiro Honda, founder of the worldwide corporation that bears his name, told me when I interviewed him in 1968:

> I am not impressed by diplomas. They don't do the work. I went to a technical high school but was dismissed. I attended only the classes I wanted to go to, and didn't take the final examination. The principal called me in and said I had to leave. I told him I didn't want a diploma. They had less value than a cinema ticket. A ticket at least guaranteed that you would get in. A diploma guaranteed nothing.

He did, however, concede that the managers of the company he had created took a different view. "If I had to take our current entrance examination," he said, "I would probably fail."

In America, a college dropout who went on to build a large food distribution business actually applied for a job in his firm under an assumed name. He was rejected as "unfit for a responsible position." Soon afterwards he sold his shares for $600 million. Two other dropouts, Steven Jobs and Stephen Wozniak, became business heroes in the 1970s when they launched the Apple computer company.

There are many similar stories; all they prove is that a degree is not essential. But consulting companies feel that MBAs help to convey an aura of professionalism and many corporations also like them.

Class Acts

Business schools have had to fight hard for academic recognition. Even now, many professors remain skeptical. But their opinions are less important than those of prospective employers.

The boom in business schools has not been confined to Britain and America. There are also more schools than ever before in Continental Europe, and the concept has spread to Asia and even Moscow. Harvard remains the role model for many of them, and a degree from that august institution still tends to carry the most prestige. The case study method of teaching, which it pioneered, has been widely copied. But business schools also have their share of critics — not all of them entrepreneurs who think that there is no substitute for flair and experience. A common complaint is that they put too much emphasis on the analytical, quantitative, logical and systematic aspects and methods of management, which business doesn't want or need. ("Classrooms," says Drucker, "construct wonderful models of a non-world.") Another is that case studies are of limited use because they deal with the past, which may be irrelevant to the present or future. But the main criticism is that standards have become highly variable. Management recruiters are no longer impressed by an MBA per se; it is the reputation of the school and the course that matters. There is a real risk that the degree will become devalued as the number of courses and products grows. The good are very good and of international standing, but this description can only be applied to a few.

The form and content of courses is rapidly changing, partly because schools need to differentiate themselves from the competition and partly because they have to adapt to the world around them — specifically to the needs of the business community — if they are to avoid becoming academic dinosaurs. Courses that fail to deliver the right caliber of students to business will soon wither and die. Most have core subjects, centered on economics, strategy, human resources, finance, and operations management. There is a growing demand for "soft" skills, such as teamwork, leadership and motivation. Students can also opt for a specialist MBA, which covers all the core disciplines but offers the opportunity to major in, for example, marketing or finance. Some people disapprove of this: they argue that an MBA is, by its very nature, a general qualification with a necessary broad base of subjects. But those in favor say that students may find it helpful to learn management skills which have a particular relevance to their chosen career or industry.

Some big corporations, such as IBM, run their own business schools. Others have sought to dignify their training programs with the title of "university." Academics naturally resent what they regard as an intrusion on their hallowed territory, and the "students" may well wonder what value, if any, the outside world will place on what they have learned if and when they decide to leave the organization. But in-house education does at least put them in closer touch with reality than many of the "proper" business schools.

Much depends on the people who do the teaching. Academic qualifications are all very well, but how many of them really understand the hard world of business? Like the gurus, many of them have never actually run anything except a class. They have not been at the sharp end of the game. This can, of course, be rectified by bringing in lecturers who have the right sort of experience — perhaps retired businessmen who enjoy sparring with young minds. Some schools make a point of doing just that. But the teachers themselves should know what it feels like to take risks which may involve putting their savings or careers on the line. They should certainly know how tough it can be to make a sale or win a contract; to deal with obstinate trade union leaders and handle the threat of a strike; to negotiate with hard-headed bankers; to outsmart an aggressive competitor. These skills are unlikely to be present if, as so often happens, the teacher is also an MBA who has gained qualifications mainly by reading textbooks or attending seminars and conferences.

There is clearly much to be said for so-called "action learning" — getting students (as well as their teachers) to study real-life problems and producing real-life *solutions*. They need to find out how to apply management knowledge in practical situations. Happily, this is being increasingly accepted by business schools. What ultimately counts, however, is how an MBA gets on in the chosen career or job. If a person doesn't have what it takes, all the learning and theorizing in the world will not make him rich or propel him to the top of an organization.

The Myth
that Economics
Reflects Reality

ECONOMISTS HAVE GREAT INFLUENCE BUT FEW seem to know how to make a fortune or run a company. It doesn't mean that they are useless. There are economists who have played a significant role in the task of finding intelligent solutions to the problems of modern society — John Maynard Keynes is an outstanding example. But the "profession" as a whole does not merit the awe in which it seems to be so widely held.

Thomas Carlyle called economics "the dismal science." He was right in one respect: most of its practitioners tend to be a gloomy lot. But it is debatable whether it deserves to be ranked as a science.

We have already looked, briefly, at some of the popular myths associated with economics and the mistaken judgments made by people like Marx and Malthus. Let us now consider the history of economics and the many other occasions on which it has gone wrong. We should also ask what contribution it makes these days, and what it may be worth. We shall find, in the process, that it is far from being an exact science and that economists are as fallible as everyone else.

History

Economics, originally called "political economy," did not emerge as a distinct body of thought until the 18th century. Henry Drummond, who endowed the first Oxford professorship, made it clear that he expected the University to keep the new study "in its proper place." He was assured that it had every intention of doing so. John Stuart Mill, for example, said that political economy should be looked upon,

> not as a thing by itself, but as a fragment of a greater whole; a branch of social philosophy, so interlinked with all the other branches that its conclusions, even in its own peculiar province, are only true conditionally, subject to interference and counteraction from causes not directly within its scope.

Keynes, who came later, warned that one should "not overestimate the importance of the economic problem, or sacrifice to its supposed necessities other matters of greater and more permanent significance."

Such voices, alas, are all too seldom heard today. Economics has moved to the very center of public concern and economic performance has become an obsession of all modern societies. The result is that, although many academics remain skeptical, the study and practice of economics is more popular than ever before. Universities all over the world are turning out numerous graduates each year and every large organization now has economists on its staff. They also have a major say in the public sector and in politics.

I studied economics myself, long ago, but became disillusioned because so much of what was taught appeared to have little to do with reality. My doubts grew during my years as a financial editor. At *The Guardian*, I saw how badly it served the Labor government of Harold Wilson, who was himself a former Oxford don. Wilson employed more economists than any previous administration had, and even launched a Department of Economic Affairs, which he hailed as a "breakthrough in the whole history of economic government by consent and consensus." Its immediate task was to help Britain dispose of her deficit and repay her debts; its longer term aim was to make her a stronger and more prosperous country. George Brown, the Minister in charge, confidently declared that "big as this sounds, we can do it." He unfolded an ambitious "National Plan" devised by his team of economists. The trade unions said it was "a framework within which modern economic and social priorities can be realized" and the CBI said that it was "a worthy and worthwhile contribution to economic thinking."

It all sounded very promising, but the experiment turned out to be a costly failure and the Department was abolished. Wilson continued to talk about a "new industrial frontier" but conceded that there was "no easy road to economic success." The plan was dropped.

The economists involved in the fiasco claimed that they were not to blame. There was nothing wrong with the plan; it flopped because politicians and others made a mess of it. In other words, *people* got in the way. They did not behave as the theorists said they should have done. This included wicked speculators who forced the government onto the defensive by "attacking" the pound.

There is, of course, some truth in this. But society does not exist to serve economics — it is, or should be, the other way round. Human behavior will always be a significant factor and cannot be ignored. Politicians want to win votes; labor unions want more money for their members; business leaders want to make bigger profits for their shareholders; speculators want to exploit perceived weaknesses. In a democracy, drawing up a detailed blueprint for a perfect world is bound to be a futile exercise.

Sir Alec Cairncross, whose textbooks were required reading when I studied economics, once said that "economists have been insulated from industrial and commercial problems, and encouraged to apply themselves to those fascinating conundrums in which pure theory is so rich." He had this warning for politicians and others: "beware of being marched in bold logic by the priestly up the garden path." It was a valid point.

The Problem with Economics

What is wrong with economics, I believe, is that mathematics has become the dominant force. It provides the foundation for all kinds of theories which often have little connection with the world as the rest of us know it. Techniques have become so highly refined that they remain inaccessible even to many fellow economists. They tend to disregard a vast array of qualitative distinctions. It makes theorizing easy, but at the same time it makes it totally sterile.

It would not matter so much if the elaborate exercises were confined to the rarefied world of academic learning. But they are not. They have a considerable influence on the way we are governed and, because they command so much media attention, they have a significant impact on public opinion. What we, and the politicians, need to recognize is that in most cases the precision is bogus and that economics in its basic tenets is amoral — that is, lacking in ethical judgment.

It is unfortunate, I think, that the warnings of Mill, Keynes, Cairncross and others have been so widely ignored or brushed aside. Politicians, in particular, seem to find it hard to keep economics "in its proper place." Many, it seems, are not only impressed by the precision but also have a fondness for discredited ideas which they have picked up at some time or another. Some Labor MPs, for example, would still like to see a National Plan. Keynes neatly summed it up in *General Theory*, published way back in 1929. He said:

> Practical men, who believe themselves to be quite exempt from any intellectual influences, are usually the slaves of some defunct economist. Madmen in authority, who hear voices in the air, are distilling their frenzy from some academic scribbler of a few years back.

Keynes himself was no mere "academic scribbler." He is among the select few in economic history whose arguments have stood the test of time. Keynes combined academic theory with practical shrewdness. If a new policy seemed desirable on pragmatic grounds, he would modify his theory to accord with what he felt ought to be done. (He also made a lot of money in the stock market for himself and his college.) His major contribution to economics was to adopt basic premises which were closer to existing reality than those of his predecessors. He argued against laissez-faire, and made a strong case for government intervention to compensate for the vagaries of capitalism, even if it meant government deficits. He advocated a permanent policy of keeping interest rates low, and put heavy emphasis on the need to maintain full employment.

This has been wrongly described as "socialism." His aim was to show that there was a middle way between capitalism and socialism. The main stress of his doctrine was not on direct government intervention with the operation of private enterprise, but on a compensatory fiscal policy which would moderate the major flaws of the system while leaving it substantially free.

In Britain, at the time, the emphasis was still on "good housekeeping"; expenditure was cut and taxes were increased in an attempt to get the budget into surplus, even though it involved the doubling of unemployment. By the time his views gained acceptance in official circles the country was at war again. In 1944 however, looking forward to the end of hostilities and determined to avoid the economic disasters that had followed World War I, the British government published a White Paper committing itself for the first time to securing "a high and stable level of employment." The subsequent Labor administrations were all "Keynesian."

More recently, of course, this approach has been challenged by right wing governments in both Europe and the United States. Under their direction, public spending was allowed to get out of hand, resulting not only in huge deficits but also in runaway inflation. Margaret Thatcher vigorously opposed the view that Keynesian policies are the best way to achieve healthy economic growth. She paid more attention to economists like Milton Friedman, whose advocacy of "economic freedom" was more in accord with her own thinking. Friedman insisted that:

> Economic freedom is an essential prerequisite for political freedom. By enabling people to cooperate with one another without coercion or central direction, it reduces the area over which political power is exercised. In addition, by dispersing power, the free market provides an offset to whatever concentration of political power may arise. The combination of economic and political power in the same hands is a sure recipe for tyranny.

The truth, as economists like to say, probably lies somewhere in between. No one wants a dictatorship but totally free markets are also undesirable.

When they are not busy telling governments and industrialists what to do, economists try to predict the future. There is a big demand for forecasts and they try hard to oblige. The trouble is that they are not very good at it.

A classic example was the publication, in the 1970s, of an alarmist book called *Limits to Growth*, by a group of economists known as the Club of Rome. Its gloomy predictions made worldwide headlines but have since been totally discredited. The World Bank said that many of the assumptions fed into the club's computer were "extremely pessimistic" and "not scientifically established." The club's claim that the mathematical elegance of its models was a better guide to the future than past history was "grossly erroneous."

In the 1980s, an American economist named Howard Ruff also made news with a book which warned that there would be "an international monetary holocaust which will sweep all paper currencies down the drain and turn the world upside down." The decade ended with a recession, *not* a 1930s-style depression. As everyone knows, or should know, recessions are a familiar part of the business cycle. Ups and down have always been a feature of the capitalist system; they cause problems but they are not a disaster and they don't last forever. Britain has had an "economic crisis" of some kind or another for much of my lifetime, but if one looks at the actual experience of most people it is clear that they have enjoyed a considerable increase in their standard of living. The world has not been turned "upside down."

You may feel that I am unfairly using a few selective cases to make my point. Consider, therefore, an experiment conducted by the *Economist*. At the beginning of the 1980s it asked people from various walks of life, including economists, to make some forecasts. When the decade ended, it compared them with what had actually happened. The professionals, it transpired, were wrong on so many counts that they were easily beaten by Britain's garbage collectors.

Honest forecasters recognize how little they really know and usually caution people about the biggest areas of doubt. Read the small print (which, alas, many of us seldom bother to do) and you will generally find that it contains all kinds of hedging provisions. Less scrupulous economists claim that their expertise enables them to make reliable predictions.

Some cheat. They publish mendacious forecasts in order to influence public behavior or to save the face of governments. In an address to the Royal Economic Society, after his retirement, Sir Alec Cairncross said that in his experience governments "hate issuing bad news at any time" and particularly "if things are worse than is commonly believed." There is, he went on, "a real risk that the government will insist on cooking the forecasts rather than reveal how awful the situation is." John Kenneth Galbraith, who has held important official positions in the United States, has made a similar point. The economist in high office, he said, "is under strong personal and political compulsion to predict wrongly." According to him, this was particularly evident during the Vietnam War. The administration's economists based their intellectually honest, but unpublished, predictions on the assumption that the war would drag on for many years and that its financial burdens would escalate. They could not, however, say so aloud because it would have contradicted the official doctrine that it would soon come to an end. They therefore made pronouncements in public on future trends that privately they knew would not come true.

The Myth that Numbers Don't Lie

THE EMPHASIS ON MATHEMATICS HAS SPAWNED another myth — numbers don't lie. They do, often. Ask any economic statistician or creative accountant.

Numbers can be made to dance to any tune you want to play. You can put favorable factors in, and leave others out. You can adjust and revise, and you can twist the end product. Successive election campaigns have shown how eminently twistable statistics can be. If you are a politician, you can use them to defend the government's record. If you are in opposition, you can use a different set of numbers to "prove" that the country is in a mess.

In this statistical age, numbers have increasingly become a substitute for personal judgment and intelligent debate. We trust them more than we trust each other, and certainly more than we trust politicians. How often have you heard it said: "One can't argue with the numbers?" One can, and should.

Statisticians commonly disclaim responsibility for the use made of their delicate calculations. But they are the people who are subjecting us, on an almost daily basis, to a mind-boggling barrage of numbers. We can't really blame politicians for choosing to interpret them in whatever way suits their argument; it is our fault if we take them at face value.

We nowadays tend to judge the state of the nation primarily by various indices and indicators — the trade gap, the exchange rate, the money supply, the stock market index, the cost of living index, and so on. Factors which are not directly connected with economics, or which cannot be easily quantified, are underrated or ignored altogether. The result, I believe, is a distorted picture of modern society — one which puts too much emphasis on material issues and not enough on all the other aspects of civilized society. We have allowed ourselves to be persuaded that economic performance is the only yardstick that really matters and that we face a grim future unless we manage, somehow, to beat the Germans, the Japanese, the Koreans, and the Taiwanese. We worry endlessly about our position in the international "league table" and any setback, however temporary, is subjected to gloomy analysis.

Economists feed the government machine with complicated econometric models and a cornucopia of other statistical artifacts. I have already noted that the precision is bogus, but it has the power to intimidate. It is not easy to challenge "expert" predictions of specific rates of output, growth, and inflation.

Playing the Numbers Game

Occasionally, however, some economist bravely exposes the flaws in the game. This is what happened in America late in 1996, when a commission headed by Professor Michael Boskin, who was chief economic adviser to President Bush between 1988 and 1992, published a report which said that the government was overstating the inflation rate — and had been doing so for the last two decades.

The commission was appointed by the Senate Finance Committee in 1995 to investigate the reliability of U.S. economic statistics. Its principal task was to ascertain whether the main current measure of inflation, the consumer price index, reflected the real rate of increase in the cost of living. It concluded that it didn't. The index showed inflation at 3 percent; the true figure, said the commission, was more like 1.9 percent. This may seem like the usual nit-picking, but the error has serious implications. Recalculating the index, it was estimated, could save the government billions of dollars in social security payments and other benefits. It could also raise taxes for many individuals by reducing the annual inflation-driven increases in the standard deduction, personal exemptions and the income levels at which higher tax rates kick in. According to the Congressional Budget Office, a reduction of even one percentage point in the index would cut the fiscal deficit by more than a third by the year 2002. It would also affect union contracts that have wage increases tied directly to the index.

Predictably, the commission was attacked by the Bureau of Labor Statistics, which is responsible for compiling the index and which felt aggrieved at the besmirching of its reputation implicit on the Boskin report. But the affair showed how unreliable official figures can be.

The report identified three basic mistakes. The index, it said, failed to take account of improving quality in goods and services, especially when new products are introduced. If the price of a new good is twice the price of one it replaces but the quality also improves, it would be wrong to say simply that the price has doubled. The index also misses much substitution by consumers. If the price of apples rises relatively to the price of oranges, people buy more oranges. But the GPI basket of goods did not change quickly enough to reflect that substitution effect. Last, but not least, consumers are able to buy many goods more cheaply by changing the pattern of where they shop — a factor which the index also failed to reflect adequately.

All this is, of course, debatable. In Britain, the retail price index is updated every year so the impact of "new product bias" is reckoned to be much less. But that does not mean that it is accurate. The Office of National Statistics has its own version of the game. The basket of goods used to measure retail prices contains about 600 items, so there is ample opportunity for faceless bureaucrats to have some fun. In 1996 they came up with a new wrinkle: they included funeral costs in a revised index. "This," said a press release, "proves once and for all that the RPI is not a cost of living index!" (Their exclamation mark, not mine.) Apart from funeral costs, the "updated" basket also included green peppers, a vase, a cigarette lighter, a steering device, spray paint, and charges for exercise classes. The Office also saw fit to change some of the places where price tags are sampled. Out went declining urban areas in the Midlands and in came Knightsbridge and Belgravia.

An inevitable result of this messing about with the index is that it becomes more difficult to make comparisons with the past — or, for that matter, with the inflation rates of other countries. But perhaps that is the whole idea.

Other statistics are also of dubious provenance. Take the Gross National Product, from which the growth rate derives. In official jargon, it is "the total value at current and constant prices of the annual flow of goods and services becoming available to a country for consumption and maintaining or adding to its material wealth." Politicians are forever telling us that it is the key to everything else: the aim of all government is to secure "growth." But the GNP is a vast agglomeration of the like and unlike, made possible only by the fact that monetary value can somehow be clamped on all its items. As a yardstick it leaves a great deal to be desired. In particular it makes inadequate allowance for a range of factors which have a significant bearing on the quality of life, including the cost of pollution and congestion. Increased activity in some areas — for example, the building of new prisons — may actually be a sign that things are getting worse, not better. In other areas, the opposite may be true. Here again, comparisons with other countries are of questionable value because we don't all use the same numbers.

In the United States the generally accepted form of measurement these days is its own Gross National Product, which has the same kind of shortcomings. GNP is the sum total of what is produced in the economy. It encompasses services as well as manufactured goods, but does not measure welfare and ignores environmental degradation and ecological disaster. When a hurricane destroys a community and the lost property is rebuilt, GNP rises.

Then there are the monthly unemployment figures, which are widely held to be an accurate guide. They tend to attract a great deal of emotional comment, some of which is politically motivated. If they go up, the government's critics say that its economic policies are cruel as well as misguided. If they go down, the administration says it proves that its policies are working. But the figures are unreliable. They do not, for example, reflect the large number of people who work in the underground — plumbers, electricians, carpenters, gardeners, maids, security guards, and others who insist on being paid in cash so that they can dodge taxes. They also exclude full-time students, homemakers, and "discouraged workers" — people who have given up looking for jobs because they don't expect to find work. This leaves ample scope for argument.

The trouble with these kind of shenanigans is that they can have important psychological effects. If unemployment is seen to be rising, many of us start to worry about the future of our jobs and there are noisy demands for corrective action, which may or may not be justified. If it falls, people will be more inclined to spend — and to demand more money.

Incoming governments often claim to have inherited a "financial mess," which allows them to blame their predecessors for the need to take unpopular measures. I have particularly strong memories of what happened in Britain when the Labor government of Harold Wilson came to power in 1964, because it had such a serious consequences. Wilson made a big thing out of the country's balance of payments deficit. The Conservatives, he declared roundly and often, had left the country in a terrible state. Most people had no idea what this meant — indeed, no one had attempted to work out this statistic before the 1930s — but Wilson managed to convince the public that the deficit was of immense significance. An obvious answer was to devalue the pound, which would have boosted exports, but he adamantly refused to do so. The exchange rate had to be defended at all costs: it was, apparently, a matter of national pride. This, as wiser heads were quick to point out, was nonsense. The issue was simply whether an arbitrarily fixed exchange rate was still the right one — hardly the basis for a great political crusade. It was the beginning of a long "battle" to maintain the existing parity, and of an orgy of self-deprecation unprecedented in British history. Wilson made regular appearances on television, urging us all "not to give up." Listening to him, one got the impression that defending the pound was on a par with fighting the Second World War, an analogy strengthened by references to the "Dunkirk spirit." It was all way over the top, and it did the government no good. Blaming the Tories might have been a clever political gambit, but it was Labor which was, rightly, held responsible for failing to get us out of the mess. As one sterling crisis followed another, the mood became more and more hysterical. The charade went on for three years. In the end, Wilson was forced to devalue after all and everyone wondered what the fuss had been about. Britain did not sink or die of shame. Exports rose and within a few years we had, once again, a fat surplus on the balance of payments.

There was a rather hilarious footnote to this sorry tale. In 1969 it was discovered that the Board of Trade, with its computers and highly trained economists, had somehow mislaid £11 million a month for the previous six years. Throughout the long and costly "crisis" we had consistently underrated our strength. Indeed, a senior member of the Treasury was quoted as saying that the whole affair would have been quite unnecessary if the error had been discovered earlier.

The lesson is obvious: statistics should be treated with a healthy degree of skepticism. At best, they are a useful guide. At worst, they point away from the truth.

One of the most absurd statistical inventions is the "average man," an abstract concept which allows economists to develop all kinds of theories. Left-wing politicians are fond of telling us what the "average man" wants, or should have. But since he does not exist, their arguments are misleading. Dr. Walther Heller, an American economist with a rare sense of humor, neatly put down this nonsense. "If," he said, "a man stands with his left foot on a hot stove and his right foot in a refrigerator, the statistician would say that, on average, he's comfortable."

Unfortunately, there is every reason to believe that the obsession with numbers will continue to grow. A wide range of government offices, agencies, and rival colleges of augurs issue pretentious — and often mutually contradictory — numerical verdicts at frequent intervals. Many appear in the form of surveys, which purport to tell us what is happening in the world but which are often used to advance the cause of a pressure group. It never ceases to amaze me how often nonsensical or absurd statistics appear in even reputable publications, dressed up as "scientific" findings.

Inevitably, they influence perceptions. Opinion polls are a prominent example. Dr. George Gallup, the father of this persuasive version of the numbers game, described them as a "continuous audit." The label is apt: hardly a week goes by without the publication of yet another poll which is said to be an accurate guide to "what the public thinks." Opinion polling has become an industry, with many organizations competing for attention. Presidents and Prime Ministers anxiously wait for the latest verdicts on their popularity. But the polls are not confined to politics; they have tended to become moral as well as political, social, and cultural arbiters.

Many people object to what they see as "trial by opinion poll." Politicians say that repeated polls themselves can have an undue influence on voters. When Gallup was asked about this, he replied: "One might as well insist that a thermometer makes the weather." But there is little doubt that polls are influential. Many voters are swayed by the alleged opinions of a majority, and polls which show a strong lead for a particular candidate or party can have a bandwagon effect. There is also ample evidence that much-publicized polls have helped to persuade lawmakers to press ahead with reforms, sometimes against their own judgment.

I do not deny that statistics can — and do — play a useful role in a complex modern society. Nor would I wish to give the impression that all statisticians are liars. That would plainly be untrue. What I am saying is that we put too much faith in numbers and give them excessive prominence. Many create an illusion of hard "reality" and can easily be abused. Democratic countries like Britain and the United States have never gone as far as the former Soviet Union, where the Kremlin made such preposterous use of statistics that they were widely regarded as a joke. (It still happens in China and Cuba today.) But the scope for distortion and other forms of misrepresentation is certainly there. We should not permit ourselves to be fooled, or to be persuaded that numbers are everything — that what cannot be measured doesn't matter.

Counting the Beans

Politicians, of course, are not the only offenders. The business world is also addicted to numbers and has the same tendency to play games with them. Statistics and surveys can be used to extract concessions from governments, or to fend off threatened legislation, or justify the rejection of demands for higher wages. Market research (of which more will be said later) can be shown as "evidence" to advertisers and others who are anxious to reach customers through media like newspapers and television. Creative accounting can play a key role in convincing shareholders that all is well, or raising new capital, or defending a business against a hostile takeover bid.

Bean-counters habitually use statistics to support their argument that costs must be cut or that a new project is too risky. Economists produce lengthy documents, with lots of graphs and charts, which purport to tell senior management what is happening in the world or in their particular industry. Brokers send equally impressive-looking reports to their clients in the hope that they will boost business. Insurance sales staff use statistics to persuade potential customers that they really must have more protection.

In many cases, these efforts carry qualifications or warnings. But how many people bother to read the small print? We accept what we are told because "numbers don't lie." We fail to make sufficient allowance for the possibility that the statistics and surveys may be based on out-of-date findings, or that they may be self-serving. We all too readily agree that numbers are more dependable than our own judgment.

It can lead to some odd conclusions. It might, for example, appear that a television game show is "better" because more people watch it than, say, a documentary. A music album may be considered "great" simply because it has made it into the Top Ten. A book may be considered to be of superior quality because it appears on the bestseller list. We may have a different opinion but tend to be intimidated by the numbers — who are we to argue with the verdict of so many?

It can also lead entrepreneurs and executives to make bad decisions. The statistics may be of dubious value, as we have seen. Research may be unreliable, and reports may be a poor guide to what is happening, or likely to happen, because they reflect the past rather than the present or future. Creative accounting may paint a misleading impression of a company's health. Forecasts may turn out to be wide of the mark, despite their numerical precision.

You are no doubt familiar with the more obvious tricks that can be played by accountants without breaking the law. They range from the inclusion in the year's profits of non-trading, non-recurring income, to calling costs "development spending" and capitalizing it. Profits can be whatever they want them to be. The tricks are not kept hidden, unless they deliberately set out to cheat, but they are not always spotted or may be brushed aside.

A good auditor will be well aware of them and, if necessary, will qualify these in a report. But if the auditors are as competent as they claim to be, why are there so many financial scandals? Why do annual reports sometimes turn out to be masterpieces of fiction? Why was Robert Maxwell (to take one prominent example) allowed to take so many people for an expensive ride? Why do the bean-counters so often stay silent when they should be alerting shareholders to what is going on?

One possible answer is that they may be afraid of losing a lucrative job or assignment. Another is that the relationship between auditor and client is sometimes more intimate than either side lets on. The auditor may have an eye on a senior management post in the company or a seat in the boardroom. But it may also be that a company has managed to bamboozle them by splitting audits, so that no single firm gets the full picture. Multinational companies, in particular, can be a nightmare because consolidated accounts rely on audit firms in different countries, whose practices and standards may not be the same.

There are, to be sure, reputable firms which would not dream of risking their reputation by failing to challenge questionable maneuvering. I am certainly not suggesting that the profession as a whole cannot be trusted. Firms can, and do, reject appointments if they have doubts about the people who run the business, or if they will not be able to audit a "significant proportion" of the risks, or if they are not satisfied with the standing of other auditors. One undoubted advantage of size, in this line of business, is that you are less likely to be dependent on the fees from a particular client — even a major company. As a broad rule, the average annual fee from any client should not be allowed to go over five percent of the total income.

Forecasts, as opposed to the audit of results already achieved, present a special problem because they are so often based on little more than guesswork and, in some cases, may be blatant attempts to deceive in order to promote a flotation, defeat a bidder, or boost the share price. There are some tough rules to prevent this kind of thing, and it could be argued that there is no need to go any further. But there are still far too many cases of dubious behavior.

One could also make a case against another common ploy: the revaluation of assets. It often makes a company look more prosperous than it really is. Everyone who owns a house knows that what matters is not what the owner or estate agent thinks it may be worth, but what someone else may be willing to pay for it or what kind of rental income it could produce. It is, or should be, the same with assets owned by a company. They may be worth more than the current numbers in the balance sheet, but revaluation can be misleading if no one is likely to buy them or if they don't yield a decent return. The figures one sometimes sees appear to be in the realm of fantasy.

Business is no more likely to discard the numbers game than government. On the contrary — computers have greatly expanded it. But not all businessmen take its as seriously as the players think they should. I rather like the tale of the Hollywood magnate who is alleged to have said: "Two and two make four, four and four make eight, and sex and sex make millions."

I am also fond of the story told about that famous Englishman, the Duke of Wellington. During the Napoleonic War, he was required to account for every last detail of his army's expenditure. In reply, he asked for,

> elucidation of my instructions from you gentlemen of Whitehall so I may better understand why I am dragging my army over these barren plains. It must be one of two alternative duties. I shall pursue either one, but I cannot do both. First, to train an army of uniformed British clerks in Spain for the benefit of British accountants — or perhaps, second, to see to it that the forces of Napoleon are driven out of Spain.

The iron duke got the better of the bean-counters, for which the public was duly grateful.

The Myth that Ethics Don't Matter

As we have seen, the numbers game raises many questions about ethics. We all know the difference between right and wrong, but there are gray areas. A politician feels entitled to bend the facts, if it wins votes, and many accountants believe that they can do whatever they like as long as they stay within the law. They do not, for example, have any problem with telling companies and individuals how to minimize or avoid taxes. The schemes they use may be legal, but are they ethical?

The plumbers and gardeners, who can't afford expensive advisers, are well aware that they are breaking the law by failing to declare their income. There is a popular myth that if you are smart you can get away with anything. The Internal Revenue Service keeps a close eye on the self-employed and many offenders find, sooner or later, that they are not as smart as they thought. But the underground continues to grow.

Employers must plainly bear part of the responsibility. They often know what is going on but in all too many cases condone it. This also goes for the people who give in to demands for cash payments. Their usual excuse is that it is not their business to check whether plumbers or carpenters are paying tax on such earnings. It is a feeble argument.

Corporate ethics are a related issue. There is no excuse, in law, for dishonest accounting, insider trading, or the misuse of pension funds. The issue is clear cut. But there are many other types of behavior that would strike most of us as unethical, but which some people maintain are forced upon them by the pressure of competition.

Business, they argue, cannot be run and was never intended to be run on ethical principles as conceived outside of business. Most executives who negotiate with customers, dealers, unions, or government officials are sometimes compelled, in the interests of their firms and themselves, to practice some form of deception. By conscious misstatements, conceal-ment of pertinent facts, or exaggeration they seek to persuade others to agree with them.

As they see it, the businessman is like a diplomat ("A man," it has been said, "who is sent abroad to lie for his country") or an attorney in a crim-inal case, whose job is to get his client acquitted, not to reveal the truth. One chief executive has put the argument like this:

> We're in a highly competitive industry. If we are going to stay in business we have to look for profits wherever the law permits. We don't make the laws; we obey them. So why do we have to put up with this holier-than-thou talk about ethics? It's sheer hypocrisy. We're not in the business to promote ethics.

This attitude — that a company's only responsibility is to make a profit — can easily lead to trouble. A customer or trading partner who has been blatantly deceived is unlikely to want to do business with the com-pany again. It may also attract some nasty publicity. Above all, there is always a risk that some executives will go too far.

Corporate Fraud

Corporate fraud is rising on both sides of the Atlantic. A report pub-lished by the Institute of Chartered Accountants in England and Wales blamed lower standards of personal ethics, increased pressure on indi-viduals to perform, and the impact of smaller workforces. Nearly 70 per-cent of those who responded to a survey identified misrepresentation of results as the main area. Such a situation, it said, can arise when a poor-performing division within a company is set a series of sales targets. In order to achieve them, certain types of sales may be "created" to give the impression that the targets have been met. Other key risks areas identified were bid-rigging, transactions with related parties, and the manipulation of computer programs.

Bid-rigging, which often involves people within a company or organization feeding useful inside information to help bidders pitch their contracts at the right level, has become a major issue. Manipulation of computer programs is also a serious problem, because it is so often difficult to detect.

Top people sometimes cook the books with the help of their finance directors. Early in 1997, for example, the former chairman of a British chemical company was jailed for two years following his conviction for fraudulently inflating the company's profits and deceiving the market about its financial health. His finance director got six months.

Powerful, autocratic men are often the worst offenders. The late Robert Maxwell lied to everyone and expected his managers to do the same. A damning report by government inspectors which examined his encyclopedia business in the 1970s accused him of deliberately overstating profits and bullying employees into going along with all kinds of dubious practices. Another report, on his private companies, included accusations of fake and backdated invoices, rewritten board minutes, and confusion between his private and public enterprises. But he was not charged with any crime and brazenly continued as before. Morality was for wimps.

During this time Maxwell offered me a well-paid job. I declined. But when, in the 1980s, he bought a business I was heading, I foolishly agreed to stay on. It did not take me long to realize what I had let myself in for and after several acrimonious disputes I resigned.

Maxwell habitually made deals and then refused to honor the agreements he had made. (He did the same to me.) His son Kevin often had to cope with the consequences. On one occasion, Robert called me in New York at dawn and told me to fly to Geneva with Kevin to conclude a publishing deal he had made. When I met Kevin, he told me that we had to share a hotel room — fortunately, one with double beds. Late at night he went on at great length about how lucky I was not to have a father like his. I said that he could always walk away, but he said that he found it impossible to do so. How he must have wished, in later years, that he had accepted my advice! At the meeting, the following day, we were confronted by a formidable array of lawyers and executives. After the discussion had gone on for an hour or so, I told Kevin that in my view it was a lousy deal. He said, "I agree, but my father has already decided that he wants it done." So he went ahead. But when we returned to London, Robert announced that he had changed his mind. It was left to an embarrassed Kevin to explain to the Swiss why he could not keep his word.

Much has been said and written about the relationship between Maxwell and his sons. Kevin, in particular, has been portrayed as a "boy" who acted as he did because his father forced him to do so. But he was old enough — and bright enough — to know better. At his trial, he admitted that he had lied to the banks. He got off anyway.

If Robert had lived, he would probably have had the nerve to argue that he had the legal right to raid the pension scheme of the companies he ran. He might even have succeeded. Juries are not supposed to concern themselves with morality.

Window Dressing

It is said that, because of the behavior of people like Maxwell, the subject of ethics (in the broadest sense of the word) has "moved to the top of the corporate agenda." I wish it were true. Many companies have introduced a code of ethics, but all too often it is mere window dressing. Codes are of little value unless they are demonstrably put into practice. This is not happening as often as it should. Many employees are keenly aware that the reward for an ethical decision can be very small compared to punishment for failing on a performance target. Senior managers are still liable to look the other way. If things go wrong they can always fall back on an obvious ploy — heaping all the blame on the offender. In America, they have a significant incentive to do so. Corporations which do not behave in an ethical manner face the prospect of massive federal fines, but these penalties can be greatly reduced if the management is able to show that it has an ethical policy in place that punishes employees who are found guilty of wrongdoing.

Large companies can, of course, argue that it is difficult to keep an eye on everything that happens. Decentralizing a business, and making it more entrepreneurial, inevitably involves the risk that some people will step out of line. But it is up to senior management to ensure that their code is being taken seriously — and to set an example.

One of the issues which has been the subject of considerable debate is whether a company with substantial foreign business should go along with the practice, so common in other countries, of paying "commission" to people who are in a position to secure them lucrative contracts. It may, in reality, be a euphemism for what is more commonly known as a bribe. Should one refuse to pay and lose the contract? "Yes" is the obvious answer if one is genuinely concerned about ethics. But foreign competitors may not be quite so fussy.

The United States outlawed bribery of foreign officials 20 years ago — one of the few countries to do so. There is no doubt that, as a result, American corporations have lost business to less scrupulous rivals in Europe and elsewhere. Not surprisingly, the United States has been leading an aggressive campaign to crack down on bribery and corruption. It wants to see an international treaty and legislation by member states to criminalize the payment of kickbacks, end their tax deductibility, and subject companies to more strict financial disclosures. France and Germany have harbored reservations, arguing that it will be difficult to establish rules respected by all. But Japan and others strongly support the move, which is sensible and overdue.

Another controversial issue is industrial espionage. Many companies see nothing wrong with trying to penetrate the secrets of their competitors. A whole branch of the electronics industry has grown around this trend, providing equipment to make espionage easier — and to counter it. It isn't ethical, but it can be done without breaking the law.

It highlights one of the main problems: ethics is an umbrella term that covers a wide range of different subjects. This is reflected in the divergence of what an ethical policy means to one company and what it means to another. Few go as far as the Co-op Bank, which has a 14-point list of pledges on banking practices. It will not lend to oppressive regimes, the arms industry, or businesses that harm the environment. It will not speculate against the pound or provide financial services to tobacco manufacturers, factory farming, the fur trade and blood sports are also specifically excluded. This may seem admirable — indeed, I think it is. But the bank's example has not been widely followed.

There is also said to be a new army of "ethical investors" — people who will not invest in companies involved in morally questionable activities such as arms manufacturing. But an extensive study funded by the Economic and Social Research Council at Bath University, which has no ax to grind, showed that "ethical investors" are only prepared to make limited financial sacrifices to appease their consciences. Nearly all of those questioned put their money in companies involved in deforestation and making weapons. The main reason why they did not give stronger backing to ethical funds, the study said, was that they did not expect them to perform well.

Another research organization, Mintel, examined the claim that there has been a big rise in the number of "green" consumers. It found, in fact, that the percentage of people who buy environmentally friendly products has remained fairly static since 1990.

Given my doubts about the value of surveys, I have no intention of accepting such findings at face value. But I am equally reluctant to believe that concern with ethics has become a top priority. There is still a yawning gap between what people say and what they do.

In business, many managers choose not to report unethical behavior because they fear that they will be ostracized if they do so. No one likes snitches. Some may even be sacked for saddling their employers with unnecessary embarrassment. It is often safer to pay lip-service to the code but to remain silent when someone is seen to transgress.

One would like to think that all this will change as we move into the 21st century — that individuals, as well as companies, will show a greater willingness to recognize the importance of ethics. There is a good chance that it will happen. The study of corporate ethics is one of the fastest-growing areas in management theory. There are over 500 courses on the subject in American business schools, and in Britain Anita Roddick of The Body Shop, a cosmetics company, has made waves by funding a new "Academy of Business," which aims to boot out the sacred bottom line and put social accountability and responsibility center stage. "For us," the director say, "the business of business is value judgment." The Academy has identified four main targets: social justice, particularly the effect of world trade on partners in developing countries; sustainability; corporate citizenship; and the "enlightened workplace" — how to fit organizations to human beings rather than the other way round.

The Body Shop was the first public company in the UK to commit itself to a "social audit" — or, as some people have called it, an "ethics audit." Cynics dismissed it as a public relations stunt, a riposte to allegations that The Body Shop was not living up to its own standards on issues such as animal testing. But Anita Roddick's concern with social and environmental issues goes back a long way and I don't doubt that it is genuine. BT has since followed in her footsteps (by far the largest British company to do so) and I expect that many others will do the same in the years ahead. We shall certainly hear and see more public criticism of companies which are considered to be guilty of "socially irresponsible" conduct. The charges can cover just about anything. Pressure groups have, for example, accused corporations like Nike and Reebok of making profits from sweatshop labor in developing countries. Others have attacked multinationals for "condoning" the abuse of human rights in parts of the world where they do business. A standard response is that companies do not control what is happening there, and that attempts to interfere can easily be counterproductive. But they have a choice: they can withdraw. Few do so, because they don't want to jeopardize their investments or returns. They *might* act if consumers refused to buy goods made by sweatshop labor or which come from countries with oppressive regimes. But this rarely happens on any significant scale — most people seem more concerned with getting what they want at the right price.

Some of the most emotional attacks are connected with the environment. Not so long ago this was regarded as a marginal issue, but times have changed. When Shell decided to dump its redundant Brent Spar oil rig in the North Sea it had little idea of the storm it would unleash.

Within weeks one of its sites in Germany had been time-bombed, another was strafed with machine gun fire, and German consumers organized a mass boycott of Shell gas stations that forced the company to back down. In the eyes of the environmentalists, the company had placed itself beyond the moral pale by its decision. Shell had to concede that it had been wrong to listen to the advice of scientific experts.

Big corporations are especially vulnerable because the scale of their operations makes it more likely that they will do harm, or will be perceived to be doing so, than smaller firms. This is why many are now publishing environmental reports alongside their regular annual reports and accounts. They recognize that the issue is here to stay and that they must be seen to care. But it isn't simply a matter of producing reports, holding conferences and making speeches. Words must be matched by deeds if they want to avoid more and more government regulation.

This also goes for smaller enterprises. Many regard ethics and "social justice" as a luxury they cannot afford, and pretend that matters like the environment have nothing to do with them. But they, too, have a reputation to protect. A small business which takes the view that "if you are smart, you can get away with anything" is unlikely to have a long-term future.

The media clearly has a major role to play in all this. Causes need the oxygen of publicity. Here again, though, it is necessary to ask how far one should go. Should newspapers focus quite so heavily on allegations and gossip, which often turn out to have little to do with the truth? Is advertising always honest — and, if not, are the existing safeguards adequate? Is it ethical to publish magazines which many people consider to be pornographic? No one wants to deprive the press of its freedom, but it should be able to devise its own code and stick to it. Circulation figures and advertising income are not everything.

The Stakeholder Myth

Some people maintain that the debate should be widened — that, while we are at it, we should lay down all kinds of new rules for companies.

This, it is argued, is necessary if the concept of "corporate citizenship" is to have any real meaning. Anita Roddick clearly believes it, and she has strong support. Tony Blair has been one of the leading exponents of the idea that we need a "stakeholder society." The basic principle has undoubted appeal: companies should look beyond the interests of investors. Employees, suppliers, customers, and the community in general should be given equal standing. There is nothing new about this. It was first put forward by a Nobel Prize-winning economist, Ronald Coase, way back in 1937 and later taken up by others, notably the American economist J. K. Galbraith.

Skeptics see it as socialism in disguise, and they have a point. It is self-evidently the case that consumers, employees and suppliers help to determine the success of any business. Most companies will choose to keep these parties happy. But what could be a sensible approach to management becomes a dangerously interventionist agenda when imposed by government. That is exactly what stakeholding amounts to — through such statutory devices as works councils, two-tier boards, compulsory union recognition, and restrictions on the rights of shareholders to buy and sell their companies. The sorry history of attempts at the state direction of business should serve as a warning to steer clear of that agenda, whatever new words are used to cloak it.

Charles Handy, one of the most influential British management gurus, says that it is time to kill "the myth that it is the shareholders who run the business, and that it is for them that we all work." I agree that it is a myth, at least in large corporations, for reasons which will be explained in the next chapter. I find it hard, however, to accept his suggested alternative — that politicians should turn companies into "membership communities." The *bigger* myth is that governments can come up with a neatly packaged formula which will transform a set of complex relationships into a cozy club. It is the kind of idealistic solution which did not work under the Labor administration of Wilson and Callaghan, and which is even less likely to succeed in the post-Thatcher era.

Stakeholding is a manifest failure in continental Europe today. The European social model is based on the formal representation of interest groups and on high levels of state regulation. Result? Taxpayers have had to subsidize inefficient industries. Consumers have faced rising prices and abysmal service. Companies have had to fire workers because a high cost base makes it hard for them to compete with foreign rivals.

The most fervent advocates of stakeholding are theorists who have nothing to lose. Shareholders do — and, nowadays, they include many people who own shares in the companies they work for. Millions more have an indirect stake through the investments made by their pension funds.

If firms want to embrace some of the other aspects of the concept there are ways in which it can be done on a voluntary basis. Government intervention is not the answer.

The Myth of the Happy Business Family

EVERY LARGE CORPORATION TRIES TO MAINTAIN THE fiction that it is a big united family with a single mission: to do the best for shareholders. Staff newspapers and annual reports are filled with pictures of the chairman or CEO chatting to the troops, and every conference speech includes the obligatory statement that "people are our greatest asset." The aim is to give them a reassuring feeling that they are part of a powerful organization that can beat all rivals and that their contribution to the common cause is greatly appreciated by the people at the top.

It may be true of small businesses but it seldom works like that in big companies, even at the management level. Comparatively few executives, judged by what they actually do, are in there to maximize profits. For security, yes. For status and power, yes. For comfort, yes. But not for profits if it means, as it so easily can, that their personal interests are put in jeopardy.

A corporation which really made an all-out effort to maximize profits might well decide that it could do without them. Nearly all companies have more managers than they need, and the most feared person is not the head of a rival business but the new chief executive who arrives in one's own organization with a brief to boost performance by axing the incompetent time-servers, who not only fail to make any measurable contribution to the bottom line but prevent others from doing so.

The cozy picture of a family in which everyone is delighted by the success of others, or shares in their disappointments, and in which loyalty and enterprise are regarded as supreme virtues, is a myth perpetuated by PR departments. It doesn't fool the managers, the trade union officials, and the poor bloody infantry. The chairman or CEO may welcome photo-opportunities, but in an organization with 20,000 or 30,000 employees it is clearly impossible to meet everyone, let alone get to know them. They are statistics and they must expect ruthless, impersonal treatment if the board decides that "downsizing" is called for.

Head office is the center of power and the vast majority of corporate bureaucrats are primarily concerned with their survival and, if possible, advancement. They are willing enough to pay lip-service to the profit motive, but most of their time is devoted to self-serving activities: defending their territory, battling for executive privileges, protecting departmental budgets, recruiting allies, flattering the brass, laying mine-fields for rivals, and getting others to take the blame for their mistakes.

Corporate infighting has never been more vicious than it is today. This is partly because so much of industry is undergoing dramatic changes but also because younger executives are in a greater hurry to get to the top. They are, for the most part, well-educated, pragmatic and intensely ambitious, and do not have any great sense of loyalty to the corporation or to their colleagues — though, of course, they are much too smart to admit it. Many of these "high-fliers" take a job, hold it for a few years, and if they have not achieved their goal during that time, join another company.

When times are hard, entire divisions may go into battle against each other. Marketing departments turn on production departments; the finance people turn on both. The public rarely gets to hear about the casualties. Even at boardroom level, where the infighting is generally more subtle, every effort is made to avoid a fuss. People quietly disappear because it suits neither them nor the corporation to have the dispute advertised. Agreement is usually reached on some face-saving announcement: Mr. Smith has gone for "health reasons" or he has "decided to retire." Compensation is often linked to a pledge that the victim doesn't discuss what happened.

As in the army, the most vulnerable executives are those who serve on the front — sales people, production managers and so on. Their effectiveness is comparatively easy to measure. Head office staff who are not directly involved in the business of making and selling things have far more opportunity to disguise their shortcomings. Accountants usually do well because their principal function is to keep an eye on the others and because they rarely take risks. The same is true of lawyers. The infantry is in the worst position of all — hundreds, and sometimes thousands, are easily disposed of, especially now that trade unions have become much weaker. Corporations use all kinds of euphemisms to soften the blow: they are "let go," or "de-manned," or "released to take up new challenges." The impact can be traumatic.

The Battleground

The corporate HQ is the infighter's natural habitat; the factory, or any other place where the actual work is done, is widely regarded as the business equivalent of Siberia. Visitors from head office are universally disliked because of their capacity for making trouble. (In some companies they are known as "seagulls" because, as one long-suffering manager explains, they "fly in, make a loud noise, eat your food, defecate on everybody and fly out again.") But they also command grudging respect because their views tend to carry considerable weight. So they are generally handled with care, even if they are obnoxious or incompetent.

Corporate HQs tend to be large glass-and-concrete edifices, designed primarily to impress. Most of them have little aesthetic value, though in recent years many have started to display works of art. Some also feature amenities like squash courts, and in Japan some organizations have gone in for decidedly odd experiments in industrial psychology. One which I saw in Tokyo uses fairground mirrors which allow executives with inferiority complexes to look like giants and cut others down to size. Another had the president's face painted on punchbags and invited employees to vent their feelings of frustration. But innovations like these are still the exception rather than the rule; corporations prefer to err on the side of orthodoxy. Executives proudly draw attention to computers and other fancy gadgets — there is much talk these days about the "electronic office" — but they tend to frown on anything which might be regarded as frivolous.

The principal status symbol is, of course, the space allocated to each executive. Many people hate the open-plan arrangement favored by some corporations, because it restricts their scope for showing off. It also gives them the uncomfortable feeling that the bosses insist on such arrangements only because it makes it easier for them to keep an eye on every employee.

A more common practice is to draw a clear distinction between the various ranks by the allocation of different floors to each level of the hierarchy. In general, the most senior people occupy the top floors and it is every executive's ambition to rise to the floor above. The upper parts are usually distinguished by more lavish furnishings; in some cases, they are also painted in different colors. The directors frequently have their own private elevator so that they can be whisked to the top without having to endure the tedium of stopping on lesser floors and having to say "good morning" to lowly subordinates. Many also have exclusive toilets and dining rooms.

One of the most humiliating features for many executives is the requirement, increasingly common in a security-conscious age, to show passes as one enters the building. It clearly indicates to everyone that you are of no consequence. People who really matter are instantly recognized and, more often than not, greeted by name. The greatest accolade is to be saluted by the security guards as you make your way through the multitude.

The principal function of head office staff is to attend meetings, and a number of conference rooms are provided for that purpose. Executives increasingly find themselves forced to do their jobs in frantic spurts between meetings — breakfast meetings, committee meetings, association meetings, dinner meetings, and meetings to plan other meetings.

There are obvious advantages in group-think: one can exchange information and ideas, resolve problems and conflicts, and create unity of purpose. It *should* be like a friendly family gathering. But all too many meetings are a waste of valuable time. They are not only hard on those taking part, but also on those who are trying to reach the people who are always meeting. Worse, a meeting is often regarded as an end in itself, rather than as a means to an end. The participants kid themselves that a problem has been resolved because it has been discussed and minuted. (Whoever first decided that the record of these long-winded sessions should be called "minutes" had a real sense of humor.) The executive who has the nerve to ask, a day or two later, what has been done about the problem is likely to get a puzzled response. How dare he come up with such a silly question — "We've had a meeting!"

The length of the meeting is directly related to the number of people present and, as the numbers mount, the chances of achieving anything decline. There is always someone who hates the idea of returning to his desk. So he takes a molehill and expertly develops it into a mountain. He asks questions, raises points, requests additional data, demurs and delays.

No less irritating is the character who comes unprepared, picks up an agenda for the first time and says he just wants to "make a few observations off the top of my head." The story is told of a harassed executive who arrived late for a meeting and was ushered into the conference room. He apologized to the chairman, quickly found the point on the agenda which was under discussion, and soon became involved in a heated argument. The meeting was adjourned for lunch and it wasn't until halfway through the main course that he discovered that he had been shown into the wrong meeting.

Another popular weapon in the corporate armory is the memorandum. Newcomers to the battlefield tend to assume that the main purpose of memos is to pass on information and assignments. But many are written for quite different reasons. Some are a substitute for action, a convenient way of passing the buck. Some are designed to elicit written confirmation of an awkward assignment. Others are used to claim the credit for successes. The people who actually deserve the credit may be too shy, or too busy, to bring their good work to the attention of those who count.

Some chief executives reckon that all these conflicts can actually be to the corporate advantage. Competition between individuals and groups ensures that the weak, irresolute and unfit are kept down while the strong, determined and courageous survive and expand. There may be some truth in that, but it is more likely to be damaging and divisive. Victory does not necessarily go to the best but to the most cunning. It certainly does not promote the family spirit which corporations claim to be so keen on.

Backs to the Wall

As in war, there are times when the high command reaches for the panic button. Impulsive thinking replaces calm judgment. The order goes out: backs to the wall and cut costs however much it hurts. The panic quickly spreads to all departments and everyone slashes away furiously at the imagined unnecessary expenditures. Economies which should have been made earlier, and spaced appropriately one by one, are made all at once in a disorderly fashion. Some chief executives, faced with a sudden drop in profits, lay down targets "across the board" and refuse to listen to arguments. Ten percent from all departments. No exceptions. No excuses.

It is at moments like these that members of the "family" find out who their friends are and whether their contributions really matter to the company. Every function is on trial and no amount of past success will save those which are judged to be superfluous.

You may feel that it is madness to acquiesce in this headlong retreat. You may be tempted to write a long memo to the boss pointing out that such an orgy of bloodletting will jeopardize the future. You will be right. Cost-cutting should be a year-round process, continuing and orderly, and done according to plan. Indiscriminate slashing usually does more harm than good. Customers are alienated by a decline in products and services, so sales fall even further. Projects which might have secured future growth are abandoned. Morale drops to a new low; good people leave along with the bad. Far from getting the company into better shape, the chief executive may have dealt it a blow from which it may not recover for years.

But protests usually turn out to be futile, especially if a new executive has been brought in to do the job. You are up against another powerful myth of business — that drastic cuts are the best way to improve profitability. The boss will be in no mood to listen. He doesn't want to know about the long term: it is *this* year he is worried about. Managers who insist that they cannot make cuts are regarded as people who lack guts and are easy targets for the bean-counters. They are "not trying" and they risk being put at the top of the hit list.

Most vulnerable, by long tradition, are the "non-productive service departments" — advertising, marketing, research and corporate planning. Accountants distrust them at the best of times, because it is so hard to measure their contribution to profits. When cost-cutting campaigns get under way they are directly in the firing line; they are the people whose efforts are regarded as the least important. Even if they survive, their spending is axed with puritanical fervor. Advertising budgets are cut, sales conferences are banned, market research is canceled.

Other departments watch the blitz with undisguised pleasure. They have always envied the lifestyle of these extrovert characters and share the CEO's suspicion that it has all been a waste of the company's hard-earned money. Who needs advertising? Surely a good product will sell itself? Who needs planning? Forget about tomorrow; it's today that counts. But marketing managers and planners are not the only ones at risk. The purge can — and does — affect every part of the corporation. Who needs training programs? Can't we cut down on maintenance? Why are we spending so much money on designing new products; what's wrong with the ones we've got? Would we really suffer if we had a reduced sales force?

Veterans of these blind crusades to economize will tell you that the best strategy is to lie low until the panic is over and then go on as before. But this usually works only if it is a relatively minor campaign. In a major struggle for survival the people who lie low may be the first to be sacrificed. No one is going to miss them. Your chances of getting through the ordeal are likely to be greater if you demonstrate to the boss that you are with him all the way. Say that you agree with his objectives and enthusiastically point out areas where savings can be made. Naturally you will try to ensure that they affect departments other than your own; the aim is to show that you know how to achieve results without getting hurt in the process. The primary target must be someone else's budget.

Another ploy is to invent projects of your own and then make a big show of canceling them. Announce that "I intend to reduce costs by 10 percent, with immediate effect, by not going ahead with the planned market research." Or "I will save 10 percent by halting work on project X."

A good chief executive should, of course, be well aware of all this. He probably played the same kind of games on the way up. He should also know (if he has bothered to study the experience of other companies) how destructive these ruthless exercises can be. But he, too, is often motivated primarily by self-interest. Cost-cutters are widely praised. Financial institutions, which in many cases are the largest shareholders, admire "tough" CEOs. If the incumbent is not up to the task he may be replaced by someone who is.

Some companies do get careless about costs, especially in times of prosperity. Head offices grow, new layers of management are created, inefficient practices are allowed to continue, and money is wasted on all kinds of other activities which are really quite unnecessary. The signs are usually there, if one takes the trouble to look. But there is a big difference between ensuring that costs do not get out of hand and pressing the panic button.

Games People Play

The character who makes observations off the top of his head is easily dealt with; you merely have to expose his ignorance. Others can be more difficult. Here are some of the games they play.

The Crisis Man

The crisis man is deliberately late; he arrives breathing heavily and carrying a bulky folder. This preserves the image of an overworked executive.

He then breaks up whatever discussion has been taking place by mentioning some minor crisis, which has nothing whatever to do with the items on the agenda. The aim is to focus the meeting's attention on him and it usually succeeds; the rival who has been doing all the talking until then has to sit there, fuming, while the newcomer acts out his little drama.

The Abominable No-Man

The abominable no-man operates on the principle that the company's interests (and his own) require the instant rejection of every new idea. His reasons are invariably the same:

- ❖ It hasn't been done before.
- ❖ It can't be done.
- ❖ It's risky.

The abominable no-man is dangerous because he knows how to play on the fears and doubts of others and because he has, over the years, developed the knack of making his rivals look foolhardy. He is a survivor, an executive who firmly believes in the maxim that, "if you don't stick your neck out it can't be chopped off."

There is only one sure way to beat him: let him ramble on and *then* point out that the idea came not from you but from the chairman or chief executive.

The Ditherer

The ditherer hates to say "yes" or "no"; he much prefers to make no decision at all. His usual response to a proposal is to suggest "further research" or an "in-depth study." By the time the various bodies have presented their reports the moment for action has usually passed.

The Spy

The spy says nothing; he sits there quietly taking notes and, as soon as the meeting is over, rushes off to give a biased version to his patron.

The Company Bore

The company bore tries to disguise his inadequacy by talking endlessly about the past, telling jokes, and spouting platitudes. The others get to tired of hearing his voice that no one asks to hear his opinions on the real issues, which is precisely what he wants.

The Buckpasser

The buckpasser is an expert at getting others to do the work. If there is the slightest risk that a meeting may decide on a course of action, he is quick to point out that he, of course, already has far too much to do but that Mr. Jones or Mr. Smith is ideally qualified to carry out the task. One of his favorite ploys is to saddle rivals with assignments, which are virtually certain to end in disaster.

The Miser

The miser is a close ally of the abominable no-man; his sole contribution consists of wailing about the cost of implementing a proposal. He is adamant that the company cannot afford the necessary expenditure. His ambition is to become the finance director and he often wins the argument because no one wants to be regarded as a spendthrift.

The Jargoneer

The jargoneers prides himself on his ability to make even the simplest task sound immensely complex. The aim is not only to show how clever he is but also to confuse the issue. The other participants, thoroughly bewildered by his flow of fancy phrases, end up feeling that there must be more to it than they had thought. The most effective counter-ploy is to arrive with some impressive jargon of one's own.

The Hit Man

The hit man has a "contract" to destroy an idea or, more likely, someone's reputation. He may be acting on behalf of a group of people who, for one reason or another, are excluded from the meeting or even for the chief executive. His target may be an elderly manager or a young high-flier whose wings need to be clipped, and he is utterly ruthless. The aim is to make the victim look like a bumbling idiot, so that even his friends will conclude that he is not fit to hold the job. Like the jackal in Frederick Forsyth's famous novel, the hit man makes elaborate preparations. He may, for example, arrange to have the wrong agenda sent to the target. He can then sit back and watch the poor fellow's mounting panic as he struggles to say something useful on a topic for which he is not prepared.

Another tactic is to provoke the victim in such a way that he will lose his temper. Angry people tend to say things that they later regret — by which time it is too late.

Games You Can Play

You are, of course, entitled to play a few games of your own. I have already mentioned some of them. Here are some other basic rules that have been tried and tested in numerous combats.

Hold Your Fire

Eager young executives often give their views too early and then find it hard to retreat. Wait until you hear what the chairman of the meeting has to say. He may be acting on orders from the top, or he may be one of those people who already know what they are going to do, but who consider it diplomatic to make a show of consulting others. Either way he will not appreciate an opinion that differs from his own.

Never Volunteer for Anything

The old army motto is just as valid in the corporate world. Veteran infighters know that volunteers seldom benefit from their efforts. If they succeed, someone else usually takes the credit. If they fail, they get the blame.

Keep the Minutes

Keeping the minutes of the meeting may seem like a tedious chore. But it has one great advantage: you can ensure that the record (which may be read by someone higher up) stresses your own contribution and supports your favorite schemes.

Recruit Allies

Two voices are better than one: if you are really determined to get your idea accepted it pays to have allies. Try to recruit them before the meeting; there is usually someone who will promise to support you, providing you do the same for him or her on some future occasion.

Laugh It Off

Ridicule is a powerful weapon. If a rival comes up with a really good idea — one that may win a promotion — you can undermine his or her self-confidence (and raise doubts in the minds of others) by targeting it as a joke. Smile and say: "You are not really serious about this, are you?" If he persists, home in on the weakest aspect of his case (there always in one) and make fun of it. If two or three others join the laughter, the good idea is dead.

Use Ghosts

An alternative method is to associate the idea with a once-powerful figure who left the company some years ago and can therefore be attacked with impunity. "Frank once came up with the same suggestion," is the kind of comment that will at once persuade all the time-servers that if Frank (who used to terrify them) thought that the proposal had merit it deserves to be turned down.

Never Admit a Mistake

Confession may be good for the soul, but it is bad for one's career. Never admit that you were wrong unless you know that your critics can prove it. With luck — and skill — one can usually blame one's subordinates, the government, and God.

Ten Common Reasons for Holding a Business Meeting

1. The executives have nothing better to do.

2. It provides an opportunity to demolish ideas that threaten the status quo.

3. It gives the impression that something is being done.

4. People like the sound of their own voices.

5. The head of the department hates to make decisions on his or her own.

6. Enthusiasts can be shown the folly of their ways.

7. Blame can be shared.

8. Half a dozen heads are more likely to think up plausible excuses than one.

9. Rivals can be made to look foolish.

10. The brass wants to see how rising young executives behave in conference combat.

The Myth of the Corporate Superman

THE CHAIRMAN IS SUPPOSED TO KEEP AN EYE ON everything. Indeed, all the bucks are said to stop at his desk.

They do not in law, and there is generally little sense that they should do so in practice. He is the chairman of the board, not of the company. There is no such position as chairman of the company. His legal position is little different from that of all the other board members. It is the job of the chief executive to lead the management.

One of the main reasons why this is not as widely recognized as it should be is that, in the past, so many people have combined the two roles. The practice has been condemned by committees on corporate governance and has become less common. I think it should be banned altogether, at least in large corporations. There is ample evidence that giving all the power to one person is a dangerous business. Many enterprises have run into serious trouble because no one dared to question the leader's views and decisions. Surrounded by fawning courtiers, and accustomed to blind obedience, he tends to fall for the myth that he is some kind of corporate superman, a giant among pygmies. He is all too ready to believe what people tell him — that, like the Pope, he is infallible. The press, assiduously cultivated by his public relations advisers, helps to strengthen that conviction by publishing interviews and profiles which give him the sole credit for everything the company has achieved. Ministers seek his opinions and he may get a knighthood or a peerage. It's all heady stuff and it is not surprising that, in the process, many leaders increasingly lose contact with the real world.

Sir John Harvey-Jones, the iconoclastic former chairman of ICI, has said that "it is extraordinarily difficult to replace a chairman or chief executive of a public company before disaster strikes." When one man holds both positions, it may be almost impossible. This is why shareholders should insist that the roles are kept separate.

There is clearly much to be said for having a non-executive chairman who is not directly involved in everyday matters and who, therefore, can see things as they really are and step in when he thinks that the company is going off the rails. It is not, of course, a new idea.

At one time, many part-time chairmanships went to retired generals and admirals. They knew nothing about industry and commerce, but it was argued that they knew about strategy. The real reason for appointing them was more practical; it was felt that their titles would impress investors, creditors and customers. Some of the companies they were invited to head were started by people who in World War II had not risen above the rank of corporal. These people were rough adventurers who found it useful to have a front man who was likely to command respect. The generals and admirals accepted their offers because, without a war to fight, there was nothing else for them to do.

Today such appointments are rare, partly because the armed forces are no longer held in the same esteem but mainly because the business world has become much more professional. Part-time chairmen now tend to come from the ranks of bankers and other financial institutions, or they may be people who have previously served as a chief executive.

There is an obvious case for "promoting" someone who has run the business as a CEO. He knows how the company works. But it should not be regarded as a natural progression. The two jobs are fundamentally different, and in most cases require quite different personalities and styles. A newly elected chairman who is about to give up the role of chief executive will be reluctant to appoint someone who is just as good, if not better, and he is unlikely to lead the board in a critical review of policies and systems which he devised. Inevitably, he will also be tempted to intervene in day-to-day management. It is not easy to stand back and let your successor get on with it.

An outsider can bring independent judgment to the task. He is not lumbered with all the baggage of the past. But that does not necessarily mean that he is the right man. He will have his own way of doing things, especially if he has been a CEO himself, and he may have already taken on so many other obligations that he simply does not have enough time to do a proper job. There are chairmen who head several companies and sit on the boards of four or five others; they flit from one boardroom to the next and often have an inadequate understanding of what goes on in any of them.

I have been a non-executive chairman myself, in both the private and public sectors, so I have a fairly good idea of what is involved. There is no school where you can learn this. You can get advice from your predecessor, or from others who have been in a similar position, but the best teacher is personal experience.

The Public Sector

The public sector is especially difficult. In 1990, I was appointed part-time chairman of two statutory organizations, the British Tourist Authority and the English Tourist Board. I had previously helped Margaret Thatcher, the Prime Minister, with some of her speeches and she wanted to see what would happen if someone like me had a go at the Whitehall bureaucracy, which she detested. I was put in charge of spending more than $55 million a year of the taxpayer's money, but no one bothered to be given me any instructions — I was simply told to "get on with it."

Friends warned me that I would find the job immensely frustrating but I arrogantly assumed that I would be able to break down the barriers. I was wrong. My bold plan to make the BTA and ETB more efficient met with strong resistance. The management, it emerged, felt that the chairman should confine himself to squeezing more cash out of the government, cutting ribbons, unveiling plaques, making speeches, and ensuring that the boards approved its pet schemes. To the outside world I was "Britain's tourism chief," responsible for running one of Britain's largest industries. This was nonsense. The industry is made up of numerous enterprises in the private sector and a quango chairman has very limited influence. But it suits the media to go along with the myth that he, or she, is "running" the show. It gives the press a convenient scapegoat if something goes wrong. So I was stuck with the ridiculous label.

Sadly, many politicians are reluctant to stand up to their civil servants. It does not help that they change jobs so often — I served three Secretaries during my three years as chairman. In the end, I decided that enough was enough.

The Private Sector

Soon afterwards I had a call from a well-known firm of headhunters. Would I be interested in becoming the non-executive chairman of a public company, Allied Leisure? The idea seemed intriguing, so I went along for a chat. It transpired that the institutional shareholders had become increasingly concerned about the way the business was run by the founder, who was both chairman and chief executive. They had told him in no uncertain terms that the company would get no further financial support unless he agreed to give up the chairmanship. When I met him, he urged me to accept and promised to change his ways. I was eventually persuaded to say yes, but it quickly became apparent that he had no intention of keeping his promise. He relied heavily on the fact that I knew very little about the company's main activities — bowling and nightclub entertainment — and that I would only be able to devote a few days a month to the job. The staff were all terrified of him, with good reason. They must have known that the company had problems but said nothing. There were two non-executive directors but there had never been a board meeting.

I insisted that, in the future, we would meet regularly and that we should be given whatever information we asked for. I also made it plain that the board had the power to replace him if we judged his performance to be unsatisfactory. In the end we did just that.

I suddenly found that, when the going gets really tough, there is no such thing as a non-executive chairman. You have a responsibility to shareholders and you have to take control. The next few months were a nightmare. The company was in serious trouble and had to be completely reconstructed. There were many days when I wondered if we would be able to save it. I neglected my main business interest, a publishing company in which I had a majority holding. But there was no way I could have walked away from my commitment until we had stabilized the situation. It took more than a year before I felt able to leave a job that I should never have accepted in the first place. Allied Leisure needed not only a new chief executive but also a chairman who could give it his full attention. Happily, the company has prospered since.

Looking back, it seems extraordinary that the institutional shareholders did not act earlier. They should never have allowed the founder, who clearly considered himself to be a corporate superman, so much freedom to do what he liked. The non-executive directors, too, should have made a forceful stand. It is disturbing that this kind of behavior is still all too common.

Leadership

A chairman can make a useful contribution. He may even be the smartest member of the board. He should certainly have leadership qualities. But his main task is to ensure that the board as a whole does an effective job. If it is pliant or servile it will probably be useless, or even harmful, to the development of the company. The flattery is nice, but it should be kept in perspective.

The chair's relationship with the chief executive is obviously of vital importance. If the two don't see eye-to-eye, or think of themselves as rivals rather than as partners, all kinds of problems are likely to arise.

The choice of a CEO is a matter for the board, but in practice is often made by the chairman. It is a difficult task, because so many different qualities are required. Is he good with people? Does he know how to devise a sound strategy for the business and how to make it work? Can he manage change? Is he honest?

It is a myth that companies need charismatic leaders. Charisma can be an asset, but it runs into a serious liability if the CEO is an arrogant know-it-all who imposes his will on subordinates by force of personality rather than argument.

Robert Maxwell was one of the most charismatic people I have ever met (and briefly worked for), which no doubt explains why he managed to fool so many bankers and others who should have been able to see through him. They expressed admiration for his entrepreneurial drive and vision. But these positive qualities were more than offset by his glaring faults. Maxwell was vain, hypocritical, irrational, uncontrollable. He was also a liar and a bully who treated his board and staff with contempt. We all know what it led to.

Not all leaders are like that — thank goodness. But there are many CEO's who have brought their companies close to ruin *because they shared some of his attitudes*. Corporate management is not an individual matter; it should be a collective process. A public company is not the CEO's personal property.

A bad leader refuses to listen to anyone else. He makes all the decisions without bothering to consult his colleagues, who have to implement them. He manages by intimidation.

A good CEO recognizes that he cannot be an expert on everything, that he cannot always be right, that his ideas must be open to criticism, that others may be able to make a better contribution. He accepts that his job is to get the best out of a *team*.

This, of course, means that he must have mastered the art of delegation. It involves risks, but if he does not trust his colleagues to make decisions he is either a bad leader or he has the wrong team.

Some CEOs take pride in the fact that they spend 12 hours a day in the office, work at weekends, and never take a holiday. They believe in the myth that, if you want to succeed in life, you must devote all your time to the job. In reality, they would be far more effective if they did not work so hard. A leader must be able to stand back, give himself time to think, read, and talk to people in the world outside — especially customers. He must beware of getting obsessed with internal affairs and an endless stream of details. If he cannot do this he is likely to become tired and irascible, narrow-minded, and incapable of setting strategic targets.

A major task is to define the company's core values — a set of basic precepts that guide and inspire people throughout the organization. "This is who we are; this is what we stand for; this is what we're all about." The values are usually enshrined in a mission statement, which has the merit of simplicity, but often looks more like advertising slogans. A mission statement must have motivational impact if it is to be taken seriously. The CEO must be able to convince his team that he really means what he says.

Some leaders have their own version of the ten commandments. When Allan Sheppard (now Lord Sheppard) became CEO of Grand Met in 1986, he laid down these rules:

- ❖ Develop a culture that welcomes change
- ❖ Delegate a capacity to succeed
- ❖ Articulate a clear vision and strategy
- ❖ Persevere
- ❖ Keep the business simple
- ❖ Aim for the impossible
- ❖ Hire the very best people
- ❖ Generate the challenge instinct
- ❖ Over-communicate to be on the safe side
- ❖ Keep central staffs lean

What has made these precepts effective is that Sheppard himself lived by them and made it clear throughout the company that he expected subordinates to do the same. The results were impressive.

A shrewd chairman should be able to tell if the CEO has his priorities right and is respected by his colleagues. He may have to step in occasionally, but he should never be seen to undermine his authority.

The real test of a CEO is how he handles a crisis. Does he turn a blind eye to what is happening and insist that there is nothing to worry about? Does he go to pieces or deal with the problem in a calm and rational manner? Does he have sensible solutions, and is he tough enough to do what needs to be done?

It is difficult to answer such questions until one has seen him in action. Charismatic people are usually very good at selling themselves but it is all too easy to be misled by their enthusiasm. This is why it is always tempting to choose a candidate who has demonstrated his ability to guide a company through crucial periods in its history. It may well be someone who has done an effective job elsewhere and enjoys a new challenge. In most companies, though, fire-fighting tends to be left to the CEO who is already running the business. If the board has confidence in him he should be able to count on strong support. If not, he had better brush up his resume.

The Myth of the Omnipotent Board

IT IS, ALAS, BY NO MEANS CERTAIN THAT THE BOARD will be of significant help. The CEO's colleagues may offer words of comfort and encouragement but not much else.

Boards are often portrayed as the omnipotent masters of a company's fate. In many cases, this has as little to do with reality as the myth of the corporate superman. The directors may have collective responsibility but it does not necessarily follow that they know how to deal with critical situations. They may not even be fully aware of what is really going on. In many of the major corporate disasters of recent years, the problems of the companies concerned were not clearly known to their boards until shortly before, and sometimes after, the event. Bad news was concealed from them or played down by the management and they were too timid, too complacent, or too dominated by self-interest to ask the right questions.

It is not hard to understand why executive directors should be reluctant to criticize the chairman or CEO. They are liable to be branded as trouble-makers and eased out of the boardroom. But non-executives should be able to make a stand. They have an obligation to the company, not to any individual, and they are supposed to bring various useful attributes to the business — experience, expertise in relevant areas, independent judgment, courage, vision.

In practice, much depends on what use the chairman decides to make of them and on their willingness to play an active role. This tends to vary a great deal. A wise chairman will ensure that they are kept fully informed and make considerable demands on them. A foolish chairman packs his board with compliant chums and keeps them in the dark. Board meetings become a mere formality. He races through the agenda, allowing little time for discussion and stifling dissent. In such companies, the board functions rather like a cozy club. A new member may sometimes feel that he should speak up, or at least offer what he believes to be constructive suggestions, but he soon learns that it pays to remain silent. Why rock the boat and risk losing your fee and the status that goes with board membership of a well-known organization?

The good chairman welcomes and encourages a degree of tension. It does not mean that the boardroom has to be a battlefield. What it does mean is that every member should feel free to say what he thinks, even if he knows that he will encounter stiff opposition. It may lead to a clash of personalities, but a board which never has an argument is useless.

Many investors feel reassured by the presence of illustrious names, which is often the main reason why they have been appointed. They can be very good but they do not necessarily make an effective contribution. Their best days may be long gone; they may know little about the industry in which the company operates; or they may simply have too many other commitments. Sometimes such people do more harm than good. They make judgments on important issues which are based on a superficial understanding of the circumstances and which may turn out to be quite wrong.

It is alarmingly easy for management to bamboozle non-executives. Information may be packaged in such a way that they are overwhelmed or diverted by relatively trivial details. Presentations can be scheduled to take up most of the meeting so that there is no time for a serious debate. Departmental heads can be wheeled in to talk enthusiastically about their local area and all the positive things they are doing. Awkward questions can be dealt with by a promise to "look into the matter," which may or may not actually happen. The purpose of these elaborate charades is to create the illusion that the board is in possession of all the facts and in control.

Harold Geneen, who for many years was the undisputed boss of ITT, once said that "among the boards of directors of Fortune 500 companies I estimate that 95 percent are not fully doing what they are legally, morally, and ethically supposed to do. And they couldn't, even if they wanted to." Why? Partly because "management does 90 to 95 percent of the talking. Outside board members, who are not part of the management, sit there and listen; then they go out to lunch, and then go home and open the envelopes that contain their fees."

Some companies also have a "chairman's committee," possibly so that minor issues can be settled without waiting for the next meeting. But it often becomes a kitchen cabinet which, in effect, functions as a duplicate board. It should not be tolerated. The chairman should leave operational matters to the management and ensure that important decisions are made by the people who have legal responsibility for them.

Pay

A more welcome development is the appointment of audit and remuneration committees, which report directly to the board. If they work properly, they can play a useful role. The audit committee should be able to exercise adequate supervision of financial aspects and alert the board to any dubious activities. It strengthens the independent position of the company's external auditors by providing channels of communication between then and directors other than the executives. The remuneration committee can devise a sensible pay structure for top management.

Here again, though, much depends on the willingness of members to act without fear or favor. They should not be inhibited by considerations of career, status and financial reward. This is why it makes sense to appoint non-executives.

The pay of company directors has long been a controversial issue. We don't seem to mind if pop stars, tennis players and film actors make millions or if someone wins a fortune on the lottery. But we complain if business leaders do so. The press calls them "fat cats." One reason, of course, is that we find it easier to understand individual effort than to make judgments about the contributions made by the people who run companies. We can see how Elton John and Pete Sampras make their money, but we cannot see why the head of British Airways or British Gas deserves such a large salary. Perhaps there is a communications failure here, but there may be another reason — a bias against business. Media people, in particular, still tend to find something objectionable about the pursuit of wealth if it involves making or selling things. It is a strange form of snobbery.

Pop stars are in charge of their own fate. Chief executives have much wider responsibilities. If they make mistakes, thousands may suffer. If they do well, thousands benefit.

Personally I am all in favor of rewarding good performance. My only objection is to the fancy pay-offs which are so often the reward of failure. A chief executive who has managed to fix himself up with a cushy service contract can collect a small fortune, even though he has made a mess of things, and walk straight into another job.

It is the task of the remunerations committee to determine how much senior executives should be paid and to deal with related matters. The details should be published in the annual report.

There is an obvious case for paying directors at least partly in stock, as some companies do. It aligns their interests with those of shareholders. The practice is more widespread in the U.S. than in Britain, where one-third of CEOs in big companies have no stake in the business they run.

Shareholders and Stakeholders

Shareholders have the ultimate say. That is the theory, anyway. They are said to be the owners of a company and its assets. Not so. They own shares, which gives them certain rights. The company only belongs to them, in a formal sense, at a time of dissolution, and even then they come last in the list of interested parties. They can vote against the board, and remove anyone they regard as unsuitable, but this is harder than it seems.

Individual shareholders have very little clout. If they want to put forward a resolution they face substantial mailing costs. They can turn up at annual meetings, and make their opinions known, but block votes usually win the day. Real power is in the hands of pension funds and other financial institutions. They generally keep a close watch on the companies they invest in and are well placed to make a public fuss. I wish more would do so.

In countries like Germany and Japan, major shareholders play a more active role. They usually have a better understanding of the business and their representatives are not easily seduced by a manipulating chairman. In Britain, directors are more likely to be left alone as long as they keep producing good results. It has created an obsession with short-term performance which is not necessarily in the company's best interest.

Some politicians and academics have added another element to the debate. They think that economic "stakeholders" such as employees, customers, and suppliers should be represented in company boardrooms. The concept is based on the German two-tier system, which has superficial attractions. The "stakeholders" sit on a supervisory board which often does not include a single executive. It makes them feel involved, but they tend to be too remote from the action to have any serious influence. Members speak for vested interests, which undermines the management's basic task — to deliver shareholder value.

Dubious Behavior

Boards should be perfectly capable of drawing up their own set of rules of behavior. Here are mine:

- ❖ No one should be allowed to be both chairman and chief executive.

- ❖ No service contract should be for more than a year, unless there are special circumstances which are explained to shareholders and are acceptable to them.

- ❖ There should be a limit on the number of companies which a non-executive may join, unless they are subsidiaries. I would not invite anyone who already has more than five directorships.

- Directors should be chosen after a careful search by headhunters, rather than by the old boys' network.

- Pay and conditions should be set by a remunerations committee composed of non-executives and the details should be made public.

- The board should not permit the chairman to treat it as a rubber-stamp. It has the power to remove him and should use it, if it becomes necessary to do so. Arguments are unpleasant, but silence is worse.

- Every large company should have an audit committee which has at least two non-executive members and which meets on a regular basis.

- A chief executive who misleads the board, or causes others to do so, should be dismissed. Trust is essential.

- Material information which may affect the share price should not be revealed to outsiders without the prior approval of the board.

- A non-executive who is frequently absent from board meetings, without an acceptable excuse, should be asked to resign. He cannot do a proper job if he does not fully participate.

All this, I suggest, is common sense. It will not necessarily ensure that the board is as good as it should be, or prevent abuse, but it would make shareholders feel a lot more comfortable. Even directors need discipline.

The Myth that Bigger is Better

ONE OF THE MOST IMPORTANT TASKS OF A BOARD is to ensure that the company does not fall for the myth that size is everything. An aggressive chief executive who sees mergers and acquisitions as the key to rapid growth can easily get the business into serious trouble, especially if he starts to expand into areas he and his management colleagues know nothing about. Many companies have been brought down through careless expansion and greedy acquisition. In their headlong rush for growth they have assumed hair-raising risks, decimated their resources, and incurred vast debts.

Mergers are not a modern invention. They are as old as business itself. There have been several "merger waves" during the past century, both in Britain and in many other parts of the world, notably the United States. Many of the big names on both sides of the Atlantic are composite creations. But the game entered a new phase in the 1950s, when clever financiers showed how easy it was to make fortunes through takeover bids. These raiders often had little capital of their own and were not interested in running the companies they bought; they borrowed all they needed, usually at high rates of interest, and once in control they grabbed the victim's cash, sold many of its assets, repaid the loans, and pocketed the profits. Shareholders went along with this because they, too, made instant gains. The offer was invariably higher than the prevailing market price.

Since then, companies have learned how to defend themselves against hostile bids. They do not always win, but the game has become more sophisticated. One well-known ploy is to escape the raider by finding a "white knight" — someone who is less odious to the management of the target company and willing to pay even more for its shares, including those held by the raider. Another is to pay ransom, a process called "greenmailing." The target company buys out the shares acquired by the raider at a fancy price, way beyond anything its earnings or prospects could justify. No one seems to give much thought to the employees or, for that matter, the public interest, unless forced to do so by unions or the authorities.

Bids and Mergers

Many of today's bids and mergers are initiated by chief executives of corporations rather than by individual financiers. They have managed to convince themselves that, by doing so, they increase shareholder value. Sometimes it works, but that can certainly not be taken for granted. According to studies conducted on both sides of the Atlantic, one-third of all such deals fail to come up to expectations. The exact figure may be moot, but there is little doubt that a large percentage do not produce the full variety of benefits portrayed when the deals were put together.

Two and two make five — that's the basic industrial logic. Companies are getting together, voluntarily or by force, because they believe that the sum of the whole will be greater and better than its constituent parts. Much is made of scientific-sounding terms like "synergy" and "economies of scale." There are other, less logical reasons, as we shall see, but the argument is not without merit. A merger can produce all kinds of useful advantages, especially in manufacturing.

The "economies of scale" are not a pipe-dream. But they often take a good deal longer to achieve than companies would have investors believe at the time of the merger, and the alleged "synergy" may turn out to be small or even non-existent. If size is the prime objective, a company can topple under its own weight.

Bids and mergers fall into three main categories. First and historically the most logical, there is the offer made by a company for another in the same field — known as a horizontal merger. If, for example, two companies manufacturing lawn-mowers decide to get together, it would be a horizontal merger. It may arise from several motives. The bidder may want to reduce competition and increase his share of the market. He may want to acquire additional plant and equipment similar to his own, in order to take advantage of growing demand for his products. Or he may simply want to achieve the economies to be had from pooling resources. Costs per unit tend to decline as the scale of production increases, and mergers can be an effective way of securing cost reductions. The result should be a stronger business.

The second type of merger is known as vertical. It covers the linking of firms at immediately related stages of production and distribution. The buyer may merge with or acquire a company on which he either relies for his supplies, or to which he sells much of his output. The one deal will ensure that raw materials and components essential to his basic business will always be available, at a price over which he has no control. The other will put him closer to the consumer. It may, for example, enable him to cut out the wholesaler and deal directly with the retail trade.

The third type of merger involves diversification into an entirely different sphere. Chief executives see, or think they see, limited scope for growth in their existing operation, or become impatient, so they look elsewhere. They tend to be sitting ducks for merchant banks and other fixers who earn fat fees by arranging corporate marriages. But this is the most difficult course and the one which most often leads to trouble.

Conglomerates

In the 1960s a new type of business became fashionable: the conglomerate. (The word is derived form the Latin *conglomerare*, meaning to roll together.) Basically, it is a multi-purpose, multi-industry company noted for hodge-podge acquisitions — an enterprise dedicated to proving that oil and water do mix.

The concept is out of favor now, but it played a major role in the 1970s and 1980s. Many investors thought it had considerable attractions. One was that, because they straddled different industries, these organizations provided protection for investors; if troubles emerged in one market, others could still grow. Another was that the conglomerate had essential management skills which could be applied to many different industries and improve performance in all of them. There were said to be plenty of good companies run by sleepy managers which needed to be taken over if they were to be restored to health.

One of the boldest exponents of this enticing theory was James Joseph Ling, the son of an Oklahoma oilfield worker. He left school at 15 and tackled a variety of jobs before setting himself up in business as an electrical contractor with a mere $5,000 of capital. After several ups and downs, his little company grew to have an annual turnover of $1.5 million. In 1955 he decided to go public. Wall Street was unenthusiastic, so he hired a sales force to sell stock from door to door and at the Texas Trade Fair. The success of the venture taught him a basic rule of the financial game: that pieces of paper can be exchanged for cash.

Armed with funds, he made his first acquisition — a small West Coast firm called LM Electronics — and changed his own company's name to Ling Industries. Without waiting to consolidate those enterprises he floated an issue of convertible bonds and purchased three other firms. The deals continued, and by the end of 1962 he controlled an aerospace and electronics complex that was capable of competing for contracts with any other in the country.

Two years later he came up with a scheme he called "Project Redeployment." "What we do," he explained, "is that we acquire companies and spin them off as one or more public companies, usually keeping the majority ownership, thus redeploying the assets to best advantage."

So far so good — he had stuck, by and large, to a field he knew. But within the next eight years he made no less than 33 other acquisitions in all kinds of areas, and his business grew into a sprawling organization with interests in everything from electronics to meat products, sporting goods, and insurance. It was a fantastic feat of corporate expansion, but there was an obvious weakness. The mergers required massive borrowings of short-term capital at high rates. They could be replaced by equity, but that only worked as long as there were plenty of people willing to buy his stock.

In 1969, Wall Street went into a steep decline — it turned out to be the sharpest drop since the 1930s. The cheap paper which the conglomerateurs had used to take over companies was now undesirable. The company suffered a bad loss that year — its debts stood at $1.5 billion and everyone was howling for Ling's blood, especially when he had to eliminate the dividend on the common stock. The man once hailed as a "financial genius" was ousted from the board.

Another famous player was Harold Geneen, a workaholic entrepreneur who was born in England but moved with his family to the United States and became a naturalized American citizen. He found a job as a page boy on the New York Stock Exchange and took night classes in accounting. In 1935 he joined a leading firm of accountants and during the next seven years his work consisted mainly of servicing client accounts. In the process, he became an expert problem-solver. Not surprisingly, some of the companies he helped invited him to become part of their senior management team. He moved several times, but his goal was to become head of a major organization. When ITT asked Geneen to become its president in 1959, he accepted with alacrity.

Founded in 1920 as a communications service company operating outside the United States, ITT in 1959 was still essentially that. The board of directors hired him primarily to tackle the problems left by his predecessor and he embarked on a major effort to streamline and restructure operations. As part of this, he introduced a system of tight controls. "I want no surprises," he told executives — a warning he repeated often in the years that followed. But Geneen was also determined to expand. His aim, he declared, was to double earnings within five years. So he went on the acquisition trail. His approach to the conglomerate way of life was simple: "We think a philosophy of varied industries can lead to a more efficient corporate vehicle than the traditional pattern and one, moreover, that develops management capabilities and flexibilities than no one industry approach can provide."

At first, this diversification process paid off handsomely. Many acquisitions were made at bargain prices and neatly complemented ITT's existing operations. His system of controls ensured that most problems could be detected early and corrected. It made Geneen and his hand-picked executives ever more confident that they could master complexity. Like Ling, he went after all kinds of businesses. In one year he acquired companies at the rate of one a month. By 1969 he had completed more than a hundred mergers, and in the process transformed ITT from a loosely-knit group of telephone companies, operating abroad, into an organization controlling an unprecedented range of industries. It owned, among other things, well-known companies like Avis, Sheraton, and Continental Banking, and operated in 70 countries. The scope of ITT's activities, Geneen proudly said, extended "from the Arctic to the Antarctic and quite literally from the bottom of the sea to the moon." It was the ninth largest corporation in America and the biggest conglomerate.

Geneen did not like the word "conglomerate"; he preferred to talk about diversification. He rejected the charge that he had built his empire in a haphazard fashion. It was all part of his master plan, he said. When asked to explain his plan, he wrote that the corporation's purposes were:

1. To diversify into industries and markets which have good prospects for above-average, long-term growth and profitability.

2. To achieve a sound balance between foreign and domestic earnings.

3. To achieve a sound balance between high-risk capital-intensive manufacturing operations and less risky service operations.

4. To achieve a sound balance between high-risk engineering-labor-intensive electronics manufacturing and less risky commercial and industrial manufacturing.

5. To achieve a sound ratio between commercial/industrial products and services, and consumer products and services.

6. To achieve a sound ratio between government/defense/space operations and commercial/industrial/consumer products and services.

7. To achieve a sound balance between cyclical products and services.

Not all of his bids were successful. The most serious setback came when he tried to buy the third TV network, the American Broadcasting Corporation, for $400 million. The merger was approved by stockholders, but the Justice Department intervened and he had to call off the deal. Undeterred, Geneen went after other companies. In 1972, he made 22 acquisitions. But by then ITT was under increasing attack in the press and by the authorities. His enemies said that he was running a heartless, amoral business, a grasping giant out to dominate large sectors of the economy and a malevolent force overseas. It also became apparent that he and his crack troops could not, after all, manage such a vast empire. The obsession with acquisitions and financial control detracted form the basic task of ensuring that the various companies stayed ahead of their rivals. Return on capital fell and by the late 1970s many of the divisions were experiencing major operational problems. A subsequent CEO had to sell off over a hundred units in an attempt to revive the business, in the process shrinking the workforce by over 60 percent.

Academic research conducted since suggests that, while Geneen's master plan looked impressive, diversification may not have created much value at all and that the financial reporting system used to control the businesses may actually have been destroying it.

In Britain, the best-known conglomerateur of the 1970s and 1980s was James Hanson — now a Lord. With his colleague, the late Lord White, he also created a complex organization with interests in many fields, from engineering and brick-making to textiles and tobacco. As defined by him, the company was in the business of "industrial management" — of buying or developing companies to make them more successful. He and White looked at them from a detached viewpoint, basing their conclusions entirely on the return on capital employed. They cringed at the thought of being called "asset strippers," but certainly did not hesitate to shed what they regarded as excess baggage from any of their purchases. In many cases, it helped to pay for the acquisitions.

When they launched a daring raid on ICI in 1991, snapping up 2.8 percent of its shares in a move that was widely regarded as a prelude to a hostile bid, it seemed as if the oldest and most respected bastion of British industry would fall to a conglomerate. But the plot took an unexpected twist. Through a skillful PR campaign, ICI turned the spotlight on the predator and exposed its weaknesses. Not only did ICI escape from Hanson's clutches, it swiftly set about breaking itself up, demerging its lucrative drugs arm and creating billions for shareholders in the process. Suddenly fission replaced fusion, and splitting companies apart became more popular than putting them together. In 1995 Hanson himself announced that he was splitting the company into four separate enterprises. With many others doing the same, it became fashionable to talk about the merits of "unbundling" and "demerging." The stock market became obsessed with "focus"; any company which could not prove that it was narrowing down its interests to a tightly defined core was likely to find itself punished with a wilting share price. One analyst was quoted as saying, "It is important not to become too big, because it is difficult to add value from the head office if you have 1,000 different centers." It is amazing that it took people like him so long to make that discovery.

Conglomerates are unlikely to regain their former status in the near future, but the concept of diversification will survive. The lesson of this extraordinary period in corporate history is that chief executives will have to be a lot more careful in their choice of acquisitions and recognize that the creation of value and earning enhancement are not the same thing. They will also have to discard the attitude once summed up by Geneen, "If I had more arms, legs, and time, I could run the entire corporation."

One of the most disturbing features of corporate cannibalism is that, even now, many deals appear to be based on little more than a hunch or the desire to exploit an opportunity which seems too good to miss. Some companies make acquisitions solely to prevent others from getting there first. They are so anxious not to be left behind, or to frustrate someone else's ambitions, that they do not leave themselves time to work out all the implications.

Aggressive bidding often produces mergers that are structurally all wrong. The same goes for purely defensive marriages, arranged to avoid the embraces of an unwanted partner. Many bidders end up paying too much in their eagerness to win control, or find that they have been misled by the sellers. Some borrow too heavily and then find it difficult to generate enough profit, and cash flow, to replace the loans. This is what happened to the late Robert Maxwell, who talked endlessly about his ambition to be "the biggest in the world," first in printing and then, in an abrupt change of course, in publishing. He went on a lunatic spending spree without giving serious thought to what he was doing or listening to the views of his boardroom colleagues. I should know; he bought a company I was heading at the time and made me a director of his operation in the United States. The banks were all too ready to lend him huge sums of money. The crunch came when he made a hostile bid for Macmillan, one of America's leading publishing groups. We warned him, repeatedly, that the price of victory would be too high but he ignored us. I realized it would all end in tears and resigned. We all know what happened: Maxwell eventually became so desperate that he raided the pension funds and, after his death in mysterious circumstances, the press called him "the world's biggest crook." He was obviously wrong to use funds which belonged to the group's pensioners, but it would not have happened if he had not been so arrogant and greedy. He had done well enough in earlier years, building up Pergamon and buying the Mirror newspapers, but he wanted more — much more. Everyday problems bored him and he brushed them aside, until it was too late. It was a classic example of an entrepreneur who thought he was superman and found out he wasn't.

Some of the blame, in such cases, must be attached to the marriage brokers who think up deals, persuade companies to have a go, advise them how to finance the acquisition, collect their fees, and then walk away. The banks, too, should take better care of the money they are managing on behalf of trusting depositors. They all have a lot to answer for. But it is up to the board of directors, and the shareholders, to ensure that the game does not end in disaster.

People Count

Entirely too many companies make acquisitions without taking account of the human factors. They barge in, after the deal is done, and try to change everything. Sometimes the changes are necessary — the business may be in trouble — but often they turn out to be foolish and wasteful as well as cruel. It is one of the great myths of business that the company which comes out on top must be superior because it has won the game.

It even happens in cases where a business has been acquired chiefly because it is doing well and, therefore, can bring substantial benefits to the combined operation. Such companies often have a solid reputation in the marketplace, able managers, and the loyalty of employees, suppliers and customers. The sensible course is to let a few months pass before moving in, so that there is time to make a thorough assessment of their strengths and weaknesses. If changes have to be made, the reasons should be fully explained and the existing team should be closely involved in the implementation. But bidders do not always behave in a sensible way, especially if they have made multiple acquisitions or are in the process of doing so. They think that they know best.

Fear and confusion are the first and foremost reactions to a merger. It is perfectly natural for people to feel that the upheavals created by a change of ownership will alter their lives — perhaps dramatically. They are not fooled by weasel words like "rationalization" and "the economies of scale." They know what they mean: many employees will lose their jobs.

The ones on the top rung usually find it the most slippery just after a merger has been completed. In the case of a hostile bid, the opposing board of directors may be turned out without ceremony. This may not matter much (other than to the ousted, of course) if the victor understands the business and has capable people who can take their place. But it can lead to serious trouble if the new owner lacks the knowledge and skills required to go on running a profitable business.

Executives are next in line: they may be suddenly uprooted from what seemed to be a secure slot by a new team of managers from the other company who couldn't care less about them and may not include them in their big plans for the "new organization." When duplications are eliminated, the company that did the buying usually decides that its own people are better than those in the acquired company — whether they really are or not.

Here is a common scenario. Your company announces that a merger agreement has been reached with the X Corporation. The statement is brief and primarily intended for the stock market, shareholders and the press.

The senior management is told that, yes, there will be changes but the deal will create exciting opportunities. New funds will be made available for expansion, for more research and development, for entry into new markets. The buyers know that we have good people — indeed, that is one of the main reasons for the merger. They would not wish to lose you. The board has thought about this very carefully and has concluded that the arrangement will be of mutual benefit. Please tell the staff not to worry.

The people at the meeting suspect there is a lot more to it than that, particularly if the new owners are known to be tough operators. They can leave, but most decide to wait and see how things develop.

Another announcement follows a few days later. The CEO has resigned to "take up new challenges." A new person is in charge. Some of the other members of the board have also been replaced. Nothing is said about compensation — though it later emerges that they have all been given handsome pay-offs.

The new CEO calls a meeting. He says that, regrettably, a plant or two will have to be closed and a number of employees will have to be "let go." The headquarters staff will have to be cut or merged with those of the new owners. There will be a new system of financial controls and costs will be reduced. All this, he says, is needed to make the business "lean and efficient."

The managers nod — they now realize what is likely to come next. The new CEO will bring in his own people. The duties of the existing team will be changed as part of a restructuring of the combined company. The business you thought would always be on top will now be only a division of a larger group.

A month after the acquisition everything has been turned upside down. You are no longer allowed to make your own decisions. You are inundated with directives from a department head. Visitors from corporate HQ arrive to discuss "joint objectives" or "management orientation" of the two companies. The expected injection of new funds has not materialized; instead, some of the "business units" are being sold. The "exciting opportunities" have evaporated.

If the company has been badly run in the past, you may feel that all this is amply justified. The new CEO may indeed do a better job, and there is a chance that individual will come to recognize your talents and give you the promotion you have long hoped for. But it is more likely that you, too, will be "let go."

An American friend once gave me a neat description of what happened when the company he worked for was taken over. "We got the mushroom treatment. Right after the acquisition we were kept in the dark, then they covered us with manure. Then they cultivated us. After that they let us stew for a while and, finally, they canned us." I wish one could say that it was just a good joke.

Able people usually don't wait to be canned; they start to look for another job as soon as they see which way the wind is blowing. They are the very executives the new owner should seek to retain. The new CEO does not need time-servers who meekly accept whatever is thrown at them. The company needs managers who have demonstrated their ability to run the business and who are not afraid to stand up for what they believe in.

People count. It is they, after all, who have to make the merger work.

The Myth that "Small is Beautiful"

IN THEORY, THERE IS MUCH TO BE SAID FOR ACHIEVING smallness within a large organization by the creation of individual "profit centers," each of which should function as an entrepreneurial, market-driven enterprise. Many corporations have done just that. Others have gone through alternating phases of centralizing and decentralizing, like swings of a pendulum.

Well-managed small companies tend to have qualities which the giants lack. They are generally more flexible, more willing to explore new avenues. They are a major source of new products, services and methods. They waste less time in committee meetings and ever more futile pen-pushing. They encourage personal initiative and individual judgment. Their labor relations are usually better because employees feel more involved. Communication resembles consultation rather than command. Dr. E. F. Schumacher summed it all up years ago in his best-selling book, *Small is Beautiful*.

In practice, the profit centers in a large organization often have to struggle for autonomy. The people at corporate HQ simply can't keep their hands off. They should be content with exercising financial control but find it hard to resist the temptation to interfere in everything else.

Another problem is that the managers chosen to run these enterprises often do not have the necessary entrepreneurial flair. Those who do have it are liable to decide, sooner or later, that they would be better off running their own business.

An alternative course, preferred by some organizations, is to acquire one or more small companies. Some see it as an inexpensive gamble: you never know what they may turn into. It's like putting chips on what you think may be a lucky number. Others want to diversify into promising new areas without investing a lot of capital. Here again, though, it is essential that the people who built up the business are given a lot of elbow room and remain as fully committed as possible.

One popular ploy is the deferred payment deal: the seller gets only part of the purchase price upfront and has to work hard for the rest. The final payment is geared to performance, generally over a period of up to five years. This is the arrangement I agreed to accept when I sold a majority stake in my own business. The main drawback is that the seller is motivated to maximize short-term profits instead of taking a long-term view, with little incentive to use the company's earnings to finance projects which may not produce worthwhile results for some years.

Small is Difficult

Why do people sell? There are some obvious reasons. They may want to turn assets into cash or quoted stock, so that they can enjoy some of their accumulated wealth before they get too old. They, and their senior colleagues, may be offered other attractive inducements by the buyer. They may feel that, as mentioned in the previous chapter, being part of a larger group gives them a better chance to expand. Or they may, quite simply, be tired of the struggle of going it alone in a highly competitive market. Anyone who has created a company knows that "small is beautiful" is a myth. "Small is difficult" would be more appropriate. Running your own business requires great effort and there are many anxious moments. The casualty rate is high, particularly in areas where there is entrenched opposition. A small business is much more vulnerable to recessions than a large organization. To a big firm, the loss of a major contract is upsetting but not disastrous. To a small operator it can make the difference between being solvent and being bankrupt. The small entrepreneur's reserves tend to be modest, with little room to maneuver.

In a squeeze, large companies not only make sudden cutbacks which often have a devastating effect on their suppliers, but are also liable to delay the payment of bills. They work on the assumption that small suppliers won't risk losing a valuable account by making an issue out of it.

In my case, it was a combination of all these factors which prompted me to part with my majority holding. I went through the process not once, but twice. I started my first business in 1978, after nearly ten years as the editor of *Punch*. Some years before I had launched an inflight magazine for British Airways called *High Life*. It was very successful and the airline said that, if I wanted to have my own company, they would give me a publishing contract. I decided to have a go.

Contract publishing is a service business; it involves the production of titles for corporations in return for a fee or part of the advertising revenue. The advantage for the client is access to a professional service for less than it would cost to set up a publishing department within the company. The advantage for the publisher is that, if all goes well, he or she gets a good return and a base for expansion.

Leaving *Punch* was a bit of a wrench, because it had been a lot of fun. But the pay was poor and I felt that I really should not pass up my first — and perhaps only — chance to make some real money. I persuaded some colleagues to join me and gave them shares in the business. We rented an office in Soho, bought furniture and equipment, and went to work.

No amount of theorizing can ever be an adequate substitute for actual experience at the sharp end of business ownership. I had been a financial editor and, as presenter of *The Money Program*, I had interviewed many successful tycoons. At *Punch*, I had been closely involved in the business side of magazine publishing. But this was different: my modest personal finances were on the line. I had to get a sizable bank loan, and had to make sure that we earned enough to pay salaries, the rent, the paper and printing bills, telephone charges and all the other costs one doesn't really think about when one is working for someone else. How they add up!

We were lucky that we already had an established title, but British Airways expected to receive a considerable part of the profits and I knew that plenty of things could go wrong. Happily, they didn't. We went on to launch other contract magazines and a newsstand publication. It led to an offer from the directors of a printing company: could they make an investment in our growing business? Their motives were plain. As partners, they would be well placed to secure a substantial amount of work for their modern but underused plant.

My initial response was a flat "No," but when they began talking numbers I listened more carefully. The upshot was that they bought 25 percent of the shares and we agreed that they would have an option to acquire the rest at a later date. It made me a millionaire, which was nice. What I had not bargained for was that, when they eventually became 100 percent owners, they would be free to sell the company to someone else. We ended up in the arms of Robert Maxwell, which was the start of an experience we would all prefer to forget.

When Maxwell Communications collapsed, we were out on a limb. The chief executive of British Airways, Bob Ayling, generously said that if I wanted to start all over again he would give me a new contract. This made it possible for me to launch my second business, *Premier Magazines*, with the help of an able managing director, Craig Waller.

Two years later we had another approach, this time from one of the world's largest groups in advertising and marketing, Omnicom. It had already acquired a former Maxwell company, which was having a difficult time. The idea was that we should merge it with our business and see if we could make a success of the combined operation. I have never been able to resist a challenge, so I gave it a whirl. I am glad to say that it worked out well, but putting two companies together taught us a lot about the problems in making even a modest merger a success. We could not have done it without the enthusiastic commitment of both teams.

There were, of course, alternatives to becoming a subsidiary. We could have stayed just as we were, settling for a good income. I rejected that approach because I felt that we needed to broaden our client base. It is always dangerous to tie the future of a business to one product, however good it may be.

We could have ploughed most of our profits back in and expanded, or we could have gone public, which would have meant offering some of the shares to outside investors.

I considered all these options. In retrospect, I think we would have floated if the merger proposal had not come along. The main attraction was that the deal doubled the size of the company and opened up other possibilities — getting a foothold into the U.S. market, for instance. My staff also welcomed the increased scope.

Omnicom works on the sound principle that each company in the group should keep its own identity and function independently. If we can help each other, all well and good. But there is no pressure to do so, and the financial controls are not onerous.

As we have seen, one of the main reasons why so many acquisitions turn sour is a clash of cultures. Entrepreneurs do not, as a rule, make good organization types. It starts out with the small things, such as having got used to having a flexible vacation policy or awarding bonuses to motivate employees, or cementing relations with customers by insisting that sales representatives make their calls in person. Then a division vice-president arrives from the corporate headquarters to insist that, from now on, it is only two weeks off in the summer, no incentive pay, and telephone-only contact with all but the biggest customers. What the acquirers often are not sensitive to is that the reason a little company was so successful in the first place are exactly those small things that corporate wants to change. In other cases, the big problems come on the operations side as the acquiring company tries to realize cost savings by shifting certain functions from its new division or subsidiary to its own facilities. Finally, there is the ego problem. All studies show that executives of small firms tend to be a proud and independent lot who do not take naturally to following orders. Suddenly they find that their advice and wisdom are shunned and they have lost control over their lives and the company they have built. They have to get permission to undertake things that they could do before without asking anyone. The new owners may also saddle them with substantial overhead charges, management fees, and other financial burdens. If the subsidiary is wholly owned, it may be given service functions for the organization as a whole without primary regard for profit.

I know of many companies where the situation deteriorated sharply in the two years after the acquisition. In one case, more than half the managers left. Sales dropped by one-third. Products that had once generated modest profits were now money-losers. The owners eventually offered to sell the business back to its founder for less than half the original acquisition price.

The crunch generally comes when the hoped-for increase in profits fails to materialize. The acquirer seldom accepts blame; in his eyes, it is all the fault of the managers. His usual solution is to fire them and put in his own people. But they may not be able to do any better — indeed, the shock treatment may make them worse. In a service business, the managers who have been "let go" are liable to take the most lucrative contracts (and other staff) with them. They start a new business or go out and buy their own company. Both sides may get embroiled in costly legal battles and attract unfavorable publicity.

Sometimes the entrepreneur has to get out because the company that took over should never have done so in the first place. This is what happened with many of the conglomerates, who in their quest for rapid growth made deals hurriedly and without adequate investigation. The business may have been sold because it was in such a bad shape that the owner was glad to get rid of it. When the truth hits the buyer, the original owner is dumped.

If small is difficult, why do so many people still try their luck? The obvious answer is a desire for independence, personal satisfaction, a sense of achievement, and the prospect of handsome financial rewards. In many cases, their ambitions do not extend beyond having a restaurant, a shop, or a pub. They don't care for the hassle involved in running something bigger.

Options

A classic case is that of the McDonald brothers, who gave their name to what is now a world-famous hamburger chain. One day in 1954 they were visited by Ray Kroc, an entrepreneur who distributed multimixers — machines that could make a number of milk shakes at one time. The brothers were using eight of his mixers and he thought that he could sell them more. When Kroc asked why they did not open other restaurants they said that they were quite content with the one they had. One told him: "See that house up there? That's home to me, and I like it there. If we had a chain, I'd never be home."

The McDonalds agreed to let Kroc open outlets anywhere in the country for 0.5 percent of the gross receipts. He started the first, which he owned himself, in a Chicago suburb the following year, and others quickly followed. In 1960 he decided to buy the McDonald name outright for $2.7 million. He then hit on the clever notion of franchising — the granting of a license by the format creator to the franchisees, entitling the latter to sell the product or service and to utilize a package containing all the elements necessary to establish a business on a predetermined basis. The main advantage to the franchise company is that it makes a relatively easy profit. For franchisees, the attraction is the opportunity to do their own thing, while gaining a proven product or service with an established track record, training, financial and management advice, national advertising and sales promotion, and computerized accounts. It is an enticing alternative to toughing it out alone.

Not surprisingly, the concept has caught on all over the world and now covers a vast range of activities. Fast food, beauty and health care, amusement and recreation facilities, hotels and motels, delivery services and liquor stores are high on the list of popular franchises. There are franchised decorating services, car-wash systems, day-care facilities, pet stores, magazines, home entertainment products, travel agencies, security, hardware stores, instant printing services, and a multitude of sports clothing and equipment outlets. In the U.S., more than one-third of all retailing is generated through franchise operations. In Britain, they account for 10 percent.

The concept clearly has limited potential for the operator of a single outlet. Some buy more than one and even acquire different types of franchises. But, of course, it is by no means the only way to get into business.

One of the most notable features of the past decade has been the "management buy-out." As the term indicates, it involves the purchase by managers of a company, or part of its business, by the people who have been running it. In some cases, it arises from a stubborn refusal to accept defeat. The company may be making such heavy losses that the board has decided to shut it down, but the executives do not agree with such a drastic move and decide to make an offer — a risky step because it may be based on self-delusion. In other cases, the management has turned out to be better at judging the long-term potential of the enterprise than the board and is more determined, as the new owners, to make a go of it. Buy-outs have made considerable fortunes for many people and will, no doubt, continue to do so.

Another option is to start from scratch, as I did. Many small companies perform tasks which are too modest for a large organization to handle, or which are not considered to be a "core" activity. The emphasis on focus has given a big boost to the practice of "outsourcing" — handing over part of the operations to an outside contractor. Candidates for outsourcing include recruitment, training, sales and customer service. The continued growth in entertainment has also provided many new opportunities; numerous small companies, these days, are run by producers, directors, publishers and distributors. They are also doing well in other areas, such as fish farming, computer software, travel, fashion, and so on.

Some companies, it must be said, never get past the planning stage. Potential partners may fall out over the direction the business should take or they may quarrel about the percentage of shares which each one should own. Finance may be harder to come by than they had expected. A detailed study may show that the scope is not, after all, as great as everyone had thought. There are all kinds of hurdles to be overcome before one can actually start operations.

There are some basic rules that have to be kept very much in mind. Some people make the same mistakes as the conglomerates — they go into fields they know nothing about. A common error is to assume that one can open, say, a restaurant because one has been a customer for years and has seen the proprietor making what appears to be easy money. A

100 percent profit on a bottle of wine sounds like a good thing. They forget about details like overheads, wastage and all the days when there are few customers. The reality comes as a shock.

The people best placed to succeed are those who have spent some years working for someone else in their chosen field. They at least know what they are up against. They know that start-up costs often exceed the budget, that established rivals will vigorously defend their position, that bad debts are an ever-present risk, and that business may fall off suddenly through no fault of their own.

Another important rule is to pick the right associates. It may seem obvious, but this is an aspect which is often neglected. A company must have a good balance of talents. Most small firms need an ideas person, a manager, a sales director, and a first-rate accountant. These qualities are seldom rolled into one person, but they ought to be present in a business. Your associates should also be the kind of people you can trust and who you enjoy being with. Trust is vital and a friendly office environment is essential if one wants to get results. You may not always agree on everything, but small companies can do without the infighting that goes on in large organizations. Falling out with one's partners in a business venture is a sure route to disaster.

A third lesson I have learned is that one must have a clearly defined target to which one can direct one's energy. Many people confuse activity with achievement. They do not concentrate on what really matters or leave too many loose ends. Stephen Leacock once summed up their attitude when he said of a friend: "He jumped upon his horse and rode madly off in all directions." I get very irritated by people who embark on projects and never quite seem to manage to finish any of them. They are a menace.

If I had to name the attributes that the would-be entrepreneur needs most of all I would say self-confidence and optimism. Unless you are optimistic about a business venture, you will, obviously, never launch it. Once it is under way, it may fail. But if it is never launched at all the chances of success are plain, flat zero. I know many people who suffer from anticipatory dread, which has a paralyzing effect. So much of business involves putting one's own ego on the line, and they are terrified of the possibility that it may all go wrong. Well, it may. Taking risks is all part of the game. No one can expect to be successful all the time; even the best entrepreneurs have days (and even weeks) when nothing seems to go right. But they know that other opportunities await them. They learn from their failures, but they do not dwell on them. People who are afraid to have a go, or who fold up when the going gets tough, will never have the pleasure of seeing a venture grow.

The Myth that Banks Know Best

THE PRINCIPAL SOURCE OF FINANCE FOR A SMALL BUSINESS is still the bank. It is widely assumed that bank managers know what it takes to succeed and are, therefore, the best people to turn to for advice as well as capital. Alas, this is another myth.

Bank managers are generally better at judging the pitfalls than the opportunities. They rarely have the specialist knowledge required for success in any particular field. The entrepreneur has (or should have) a far better understanding of the potential for his product or service, because of his previous experience and management skills.

A local branch manager should know something about the community and will have individual views regarding the viability of, say, a shop or a restaurant. They will be influenced by cases he has dealt with previously. But he is not infallible, and does not pretend to be. If he has entrepreneurial instincts, he would probably give up his job and join in the game.

If significant amounts of capital are involved, the local manager will usually have to consult head office, where senior managers tend to have even less expertise in how a company should be run. They are money-lenders, not entrepreneurs, and they are just as capable of making mistakes as everyone else.

The clearing banks have incurred horrendous losses on some of their loans. They have, in the past, lent billions to countries that subsequently defaulted or asked for revised terms. They have often made terrible investments. The Midland Bank, for example, paid $820 million for a stake in Crocker's National Bank (under previous ownership) and then sat impotently by as this awful West Coast operation lost so much money — $178 million in a mere six months — that it eventually had to be abandoned altogether. The Maxwell episode also demonstrated a remarkable lack of judgment.

Banks make the bulk of their profits on net interest income. This is the difference between the interest on money "borrowed" from depositors and other banks and the interest they receive on the same money "lent" to borrowers, such as entrepreneurs. The margins tend to be relatively modest, but there are possible long-term rewards. A young company that grows into a successful strong business creates a potential source of additional income — from fees, foreign exchange, leasing, factoring, venture capital, merchant banking, insurance, extra personal accounts for an expanding and increasingly affluent workforce, and increases in local business activity. Bankers are well aware of this and attempts to poach "star" accounts in the medium-sized corporate sector are legion. However, research in several countries has indicated that entrepreneurs who have a good banking relationship are surprisingly loyal to the bank which helped them to start up and that attempts to poach them are often resisted. This may, of course, change if the shareholders sell out — the acquiring company generally insists that the account must be switched to its own bank.

No one can predict with any degree of certainty which new businesses will succeed — or when they will do so. Bankers comfort themselves with the thought that the failure rates are highest early on, when the amount of debt a company carries is relatively small. But they prefer to err on the side of caution.

Banks are constantly asked to put up virtually all the finance for a new venture. From the entrepreneur's point of view, the ideal structure for a new business is one that requires no commitment of capital to secure the use of necessary assets. He wants to minimize his own financial investment while maximizing his control, defined as share-ownership. But banks are seldom willing to entertain such a proposal. If they do, the loan will have so many conditions attached to it that the banker will not just "control" the business but also the entrepreneur.

Experience and statistics have led bankers to believe that new ventures are, on average, high-risk propositions. It is difficult to make a reliable assessment of the true abilities of an entrepreneur and the real prospects for the proposed project. Having provided finance, a bank may also find it hard to ascertain whether the entrepreneur is actually devoting enough effort to ensuring its success. This is why banks are so anxious to have security in support of a loan. Collateral provides a mean of recovering at least some of their investment should the venture fail, and its realizable value should be greater than or equal to the value of the loan. This can present problems, particularly in relation to business assets. In the event of a default these usually command a much lower price (at auction for example) than their value to the company as a going concern. Often the main fall-back security available at start-up is a personal guarantee backed by assets, such as the family home.

The practice of requesting personal guarantees varies from country to country. Entrepreneurs hate them because they wipe out the advantage of limited liability. Bankers like them because they feel that the entrepreneur will work that much harder to ensure the loan is repaid. Even if the entrepreneur is willing to guarantee the whole loan with personal assets, the bank will expect the individual to put some equity into the business, most likely equal to 25 percent of the amount of the loan.

This is where it gets scary; you may end up with all your personal net worth tied up in the same business that provides all your income. If the venture flops, you lose both your savings and means of support. Seen objectively, such risks seem only justified if the profit potential is high enough to yield a commensurate return. As a rough rule of thumb, you must believe that it is possible to multiply your original investment by a factor of 10. But you cannot be sure how the venture will turn out; starting a business is an act of faith.

Your associates, of course, should be willing to chip in. In many cases, equity capital also comes from close friends and relatives.

My contacts in the banking world say that many people who go into business for the first time do not understand the nature of lending. But it is clearly important to see a proposal from the banker's point of view.

Personal loans are routinely screened in many countries using computerized credit scoring techniques. Commercial loan decisions, in contrast, are still heavily influenced by the impression made by the entrepreneur. The financially literate and articulate borrower has a real competitive advantage in the market for debt finance. The most obvious requirement is a well-prepared business plan. Without it, one is likely to walk away empty-handed. The banker may not be able to understand or judge all the details, but at least will see that the applicant has done the needed homework. In the interview, the loan officer will probably question key assumptions behind the numbers, which can be helpful. The bankers will also be influenced by the applicant's track record; someone with a past failure is bound to encounter much greater skepticism than someone who has already had some success.

Bankers often have simple checklists. Here are two that are widely used:

1. *The 5 Cs*

    Character of borrower

    Capacity to repay

    Conditions (product, industry, economy)

    Capital provided (debt/equity ratio)

    Collateral, or security

2. *Campari*

    Character of borrower

    Ability to borrow and repay

    Margin to profit

    Purpose of the loan

    Amount of the loan

Repayment terms

Insurance against non-payment

Some have introduced more complex checklists that are closer to credit-scoring systems. Opinions vary as to the value for new venture proposals; many bankers place more weight on their judgment of how the entrepreneur will cope in any eventuality.

When I went into business, my earlier experience as a financial journalist proved to be useful. I had spent years analyzing the balance sheets of other companies; I had interviewed many successful people; I knew a lot about the pitfalls; and I had met many bankers. So when I approached my own bank I had a fair idea of what kind of questions to expect. I took the precaution of writing a business plan, and as already mentioned, I had a publishing deal with British Airways in my pocket. Nevertheless, the bank demanded a personal guarantee. I was willing enough to give it (my partners were not) but my assets were modest and I was only offered a small overdraft. So I went to a large firm of printers and asked if they would provide an additional guarantee if I gave them a contract to print *High Life*. They said yes, the bank was happy, and I got what I wanted. I also managed to secure a substantial line of credit from the people who supplied our paper. As things turned out, we never actually had to use the overdraft but it was comforting to know that it was there.

The main drawback to a close association with a supplier is that it limits one's room for maneuver; if someone else comes along with better terms, one ought to be in a position to accept. But arrangements of this kind are by no means uncommon.

Angels and Vultures

Because bankers are so cautious in their attitude towards new ventures, there is always the possibility that your application will be rejected. You can go to other banks, but the same thing may happen. It is such a discouraging experience that you may feel like giving up at this point. But there are other options.

You may be able to find a wealthy investor who will put up some capital in return for a share stake. Such people, widely known as "angels," often have substantial business experience and are better at judging the merits of a proposal than bank managers.

Angels are not as philanthropic as their nickname suggests. They know the risks and they are tough. Most of them keep a low profile. They are not listed in any directory and there is no official record of their investments. Making generalizations about them and their activity is problematic. But their numbers have grown considerably in recent years and it is worth asking friends or business contacts if they know of anyone who might be interested in your venture.

Studies undertaken in the UK and North America suggest that angel investments have several main characteristics. The majority invest less than $75,000 in each project, although some will provide more than $150,000 per deal. Half involve co-investors, usually trusted associates. They will sometimes provide additional follow-on capital. Their support can also help in negotiations with banks.

Most of their investments are local, typically within 50 to 100 miles of where they live. They usually involve equity finance. Angels seldom take a controlling interest, but they may add value by contributing their commercial skills. They are fairly patient investors, with a majority willing to hold their shares for more than five years. They are motivated first and foremost by the opportunity for capital gain, so they are only interested in businesses that have the potential to achieve profitable growth — that will generate returns of 30 percent or more a year (averaged over the life of an investment) on start-ups and at least 20 percent for investments in established companies. It is a tall order, which is why many proposals for angel funding are turned down at the initial screening stage. But angels are usually quick to make decisions and, once committed, can be very useful allies.

Andrew Lloyd Webber once told me that, in his earlier days, he managed to get hold of a list of angels circulating in London's theater land. "A lot of them were doctors and dentists," he said. Without their money some of his musicals might never have seen the light of day. They took a chance — and he made them rich. "Cats" has so far returned $45,000 plus the original stake for every $1,500 invested in 1981. It's that potential for gain which continues to attract investors. The Society of London Theaters receives up to 60 letters a day from people asking for details of plays and musicals which need backers. But spectacular misses are more frequent than hits. Informal estimates suggest that angels can expect total losses on two out of five productions, two breaking even, and one making good money.

My friend Keith Waterhouse, who has written successful plays of his own, once tried to devise a rule of conduct. He resolved never to invest in a musical unless it had a reasonably coherent script and at least one big star. When he was asked to put some money into an American rock musical about a gang of hippies he turned the proposal down without a moment's hesitation. The script was sketchy, the plot non-existent, and it was proposed to launch this flimsy vehicle with a cast of complete unknowns. Who would want to see a show about hippies, except other hippies? Plenty of people, it turned out. The musical was "Hair," and it was a hit. Another friend of mine, following the same rules, invested in a thriller with three TV stars and a good final twist — he lost his shirt.

Movies are just as risky. The popular notion that they are a good way to make a fortune is a myth. Filmmakers are always on the lookout for backers and they talk persuasively about percentages, tax-shelter deals, and other supposed advantages. But seven out of ten films lose money. As with the theater, it is the tantalizing possibility of a lucky strike that keeps producers going and investors interested. Remember *Easy Rider*? It started out as a cult movie and became a generational event. For an investment of $300,000 it returned over $35 million.

But even if a film is a hit, an angel may make very little after everyone else has taken a cut. As Hollywood legend has it: "a backer is an angel, but an angel is a sucker." This is why most serious investors prefer to stick to fields they know and entrepreneurs they can trust.

Sometimes an offer can come out of the blue. This is what happened to David Lloyd, the tennis player. When he played the professional circuit, he traveled to different parts of the world where tennis clubs were popular. He decided, when he left the pro game, to launch a chain of similar clubs in Britain. He found a piece of land near London's airport, invested all his money earned from tennis, and tried to raise the rest of the finance for the project. The banks were negative; he kept knocking on doors to no avail. Finally Barratts, the builders, were interested but wanted 50 percent. Lloyd did not want to give away half of the club but he was considering the deal when someone phoned him out of the blue and said, "Look, I've got some money to invest. I love tennis." By the mid-1990s he had 13 clubs, with an annual turnover of $40 million and was able to float his company on the stock market. He later sold his shares to Whitbread in a deal which netted him $35 million. The angel also made a handsome profit.

Another option is to look for help from formal venture capital companies. They are sophisticated equity investors who, like angels, are chiefly after capital gain. The banks are nowadays involved in this kind of business, through separate units, but there are many independent firms which spend a great deal of time screening business ventures for appropriate opportunities. As many as a 100 may be reviewed before one is selected for investment.

Entrepreneurial folklore says that professional venture capitalists do not invest in a company until their rising greed overcomes their declining fear. In other words, they do not put money into a company until they are convinced that there is a reasonable probability that the financial returns measure up to the risk. They generally expect to get a return of between five and ten times their initial investment in about five to seven years. In an ideal case the company will grow rapidly and float an initial public offering of its shares within five years of the first venture capital investment, or sell the business to a larger group.

In practice, this means that venture capitalists will only back companies with first-class entrepreneurial leaders in markets that are big enough for a company's sales to show significant growth in sales and profits. They also like to hedge their bets by providing the finance in stages and syndicating the deal with other venture firms. The risk can be further reduced by purchasing convertible preferred shares, which give them specific rights and preferences compared with holders of ordinary shares.

One of the principal drawbacks in getting involved with these people is that their investments tend to have numerous covenants and restrictions. When things go badly wrong, they exercise their rights and intervene in managing the company, often removing one or more of the founding entrepreneurs. It is these situations which have given rise to the derogatory term "vulture capitalists." However, when things go well, everyone wins.

In Britain they have tended to focus increasingly on management buyouts of all or part of a business, because they are usually more profitable than start-up companies and pay off more quickly. John Moulton, one of the doyens of the game, claims to have made 110 millionaires so far in his career and to have accumulated a large personal fortune in the process. Others have also done well, but there are plenty of pitfalls. The idea that venture capitalism is an easy path to wealth is another myth. Like the banks, the players are liable to make serious errors of judgment. Much also depends on the state of the economy and the stock market. In the last recession many companies went bust; the most frequent exit route for the people who had financed them was the receiver.

In America, venture capitalists tend to be much bolder. They are more inclined to finance start-up and early-stage businesses. Without them famous names like Microsoft, Apple Computers, America Online and Netscape would never have got off the drawing board. At times they are instrumental in the creation of the companies they back, bringing together entrepreneurs and technologists to launch new enterprises. High tech predominates and the returns are often phenomenal. In 1994, for example, the head of a partnership in California's Silicon Valley, John Doerr, invested $5 million in backing the Internet firm Netscape. By 1995 the value of that investment had grown to a staggering $400 million.

Venture capital is at the heart of Silicon Valley. Californian financiers are prepared to take a Darwinian view of business: invest in a lot and let the fittest survive. It is not unusual for only one or two companies in a portfolio to make it to success. For every Netscape there are many enterprises that have tried to do the same and failed. But the profits on the winners can be so big that it is reckoned to be worth taking the risk.

Myths about Entrepreneurs

One of the most intriguing aspects of Silicon Valley is the abundance of "serial entrepreneurs" — people who have created and sold several companies. They get an idea, launch a business, see it through its early stages, and then move on.

Some of these characters are like the juggler in a circus act who starts one plate spinning on a stick, then another, then a third. By this time, the first plate needs some help to keep going. Now he starts a fourth plate spinning and gives some needed attention to the others. He has to keep moving around to make sure that they all perform. Management bores such people; it's the act that counts.

The Valley's entrepreneurial environment is conducive to this kind of behavior. There is less stigma attached to failure than in countries like Britain. If you leave a solid job in a high-tech firm to start your own business and it does not work out, getting another job will not be difficult. So more people tend to have a go.

An entrepreneur is someone who makes things happen. Most of the great corporations today were started by one person who followed through on an idea. Bill Gates of Microsoft is a prominent example.

The term "entrepreneur" has long been taken to mean an individual who is vital, creative, courageous. There is something that sets this type apart from the crowd. One of the most powerful motivations is independence. An entrepreneur does not want to be told what to do by other people, including government officials. The firm is a projection of the entrepreneur and is a form of self-expression. He is the king-pin of the enterprise and wants to be left alone.

Some of these people start small and remain small. There is a difference between the person who runs the local grocery store and the entrepreneur who builds a chain of them. The shopkeeper is more interested in independence than achievement. The builder has more lofty ambitions, takes risks, and is not easily put off by setbacks and upsets. But both have a common desire: to be in control. Neither feels comfortable in a big organization run by someone else.

Publishing has always attracted entrepreneurial types. Philip Kogan, the publisher of this book, started his business 30 years ago and has held on to it. He says:

> A number of my contemporaries sold out and wish they hadn't. The main concern of a purchaser is to use the acquisition to help pay for his overhead superstructure — warehousing, sales representation and the like. Having absorbed what is essentially a creative unit, which might or might not happen to an efficient firm, he then ignores the very thing that brought it into existence in the first place — the generation of new ideas and products. So the product flow dries up and the suits move in and take away the identity of the victim. This process has led to many fine independent imprints being first thrown around like shuttlecocks between multinational predators and then being shut down or sold off cheaply.

I can well understand why people like Philip have been determined to remain in charge. It is painful to see that kind of thing happen to a business you care for.

The most widely recognized definition of an entrepreneur is "someone who is in business for himself." But nowadays it is often used to describe any professional who shows initiative. Because of this, several myths have gained acceptance.

One is that entrepreneurship can be taught. Many colleges have "professors of entrepreneurship" who claim to have all the answers. Anita Roddick, founder of The Body Shop, is among the many people at the sharp end of business who question this assumption. She asks:

> How do you teach obsession? There is a fine line between the delinquent mind of an entrepreneur and that of a crazy person. The entrepreneur's dream is almost a kind of madness, and it is almost as isolating. When you see something new, your vision usually isn't shared by others. The difference between a crazy person and the successful entrepreneur is that the latter can convince others to share the vision. That force of will is fundamental to entrepreneurship.

What could a professor know about the "force of will?" The professor can conduct numerous case studies, and devise fancy theories, but how can an academic truly understand — let alone convey — the "kind of madness" that makes all the difference?

The argument that we can all be entrepreneurs if we go to the right school, has led to the myth that the "entrepreneurial spirit" can easily be introduced into large corporations and even government. But, as we have seen, big business tends to find it difficult to accommodate independent-minded and often awkward people. This is even more true of government.

It has become fashionable among academics to talk about the "social entrepreneur." According to them, the social entrepreneur's rewards "do not include personal wealth-creation." The motive is to increase "soci-etal wealth" — better health care, education and welfare services. In return the individual can expect "personal recognition, professional rewards, enhanced influence, and status within the community."

It sounds both reasonable and noble, but it is a myth. There is, obvious-ly, much to be said for making public services more efficient. Bringing in people from the private sector makes a lot of sense. But they tend to be *managers*, not entrepreneurs.

The public sector requires a different set of attributes. There is no green field, no debt-raising exercise, no diverting acquisition. The future has always to be built on the foundations of the past. It calls for talents which even the most successful entrepreneur usually finds too difficult to muster. Political control, public accountability, and the role of the civil servant fit in awkwardly with his basic premise.

Success or failure for the private entrepreneur will usually touch few lives outside the immediate family and staff. In the average "social business" it will be both public and affect the lives of many. Failure, both personal and organizational, may arise from factors generally unknown in the private sector — from the exercise of self-interest on the part of the vocational professionals, from political interference, and from the expression of public disquiet, so eagerly picked up by the media. Past success is no pro-tection; indeed, it may only enhance future vulnerability.

The entrepreneur is expected to handle all this on a salary which is mea-ger compared with the money to be earned in the private sector. The public sector leader must forget about capital gain — the objective of most business ventures. It is hardly an appealing prospect for ambitious individuals. They may be tempted by the challenge, but they usually end up so frustrated that they leave. It happened to me.

Less is More

I suspect that the people who invented the concept of the "social entre-preneur" are primarily concerned with defending, and if possible enhancing, the role of the public sector. Many have never accepted the Thatcherite view that we need less government — that we are likely to get more and better services if the private sector takes over responsibil-ity for them. They acknowledge that an injection of commercial disci-pline has been useful, but think that the State should continue to play Nanny.

The evidence is against them. Margaret Thatcher did both taxpayers and customers a favor when she privatized industries that used to be owned by the State. Many lost vast amounts of money and provided abysmal ser-vices. She decided that government could not run business enterprises and refused to have anything to do with schemes that amounted to little more than tinkering. She did not believe that civil servants could be turned into entrepreneurs and she was right. Companies like British Airways were transformed by people with genuine entrepreneurial flair who were given a free hand. No sensible person could reasonably argue today that they would have done better if they had remained in public ownership. Many politicians, however, have yet to come to terms with the obvious conclusion: that they should play a limited role. They want to be in charge and, of course, they are supported in this by the bureaucracy.

There is clearly a need for *some* control. The private sector cannot be allowed to do whatever it likes. But this does not mean that government should interfere in every aspect of business.

One of the most popular myths is that much can be achieved by the cre-ation of new agencies. Politicians are forever coming up with "new ideas," which they imagine will solve whatever problems they think need to be tackled. So we have all kinds of elaborate schemes, usually produced by people who have little or no practical business experience. Some are supposed to cure unemployment; some are meant to help small companies; some allegedly make business more efficient. The taxpayer's money is freely spent on "initiatives" which all too often turn out to be futile. Politicians should protect us from this nonsense, not promote it, and the media should surely make a greater effort to discover the truth.

Entrepreneurs do not need governments to tell them what to do, or how to do it, any more that they need professors and other management gurus. They will naturally take advantage of any financial assistance that may be on offer but what they want above all is maximum freedom to do their own thing. As they see it, politicians would be more usefully occupied in tackling red tape.

Last, but not least, there are the merchant banks — or investment banks, as they are called in America. Don't bother to go to them for start-up capital. Their main interest, as noted previously, is in lucrative deals. They will arrange underwriting and mergers, but they like to talk big numbers. They are the people to see once you have made it to the major league.

The banking world has been much criticized for its apparent obsession with security and short-term performance. Much has been made of the contrasting experience of Anglo-Saxon methods in the UK and the U.S. and the more relationship-based "industrial banking" approach, such as that operated in countries like Germany and Japan. I think the criticism is justified. I have served for some years on the board of Thomas Cook, which has been owned, in turn, by a British and a German bank. I prefer the German approach, which engenders a longer-term perspective on the growth and development of businesses as well as a more highly qualified bank staff. My boardroom colleagues are people who not only understand banking but also make a point of getting closely involved in the companies they invest in. This is welcomed by the management and I would like to believe that, in time, British and American banks will come to appreciate the value of making the same kind of commitment.

T·H·I·R·T·E·E·N

The Myth that
"Pioneering Don't Pay"

BEAN-COUNTERS TEND TO HAVE A PARTICULARLY DIFFICULT relationship with creative people. They are inclined to see them as frivolous, irresponsible spendthrifts who waste the company's hard-earned money on fanciful projects.

There is nothing new about this. Some years ago I wrote a book called *The Innovators*, which looked at the remarkable careers of more than a hundred people who have made things happen in the 20th century. Most of them, I found, encountered the same kind of objections one still hears today, "It can't be done. It costs too much. It's too risky. It takes too long to get returns."

Warren Avis, who developed the airport car rental concept while still in his twenties, recalled that the objections "ran the gamut of negative thinking. I was told that a national car-rental system of this type would be impossible to control. There would not be enough demand from business travelers. The cost of buying and maintaining the cars would undermine any profitability. You name it, the naysayers threw it at me." Sir Alistair Pilkington who developed the "float" method of glass-making, said that he struggled for seven years to prove that his theories had any practical value. The bean-counters kept asking him, "When will you succeed?" All he could say was, "We will know the answer to that only when we have succeeded." His process eventually made all the existing ways of making plate glass obsolete, and the company earned many millions from licensing fees.

Ross Perot, who has since gained fame as a political maverick in the U.S., worked for IBM as a salesman when he had the bright idea that the company should create a service organization that would design, install, and operate electronic data processing systems on a fixed contract basis. IBM told him that the concept was absurdly impractical, so he left and started his own business with $1,000 of savings. When the company went public six years later he became a multi-millionaire.

Walt Disney found it so hard to get financial backing for his dreams that his first business venture ended in bankruptcy. In meetings with skeptical bankers he used to act out all the parts of a Mickey Mouse or Donald Duck scenario; one can imagine their reaction.

Here are some other true stories.

> When the Ford Motor Company was launched, the president of the Michigan Savings Bank advised Henry Ford's lawyer not to invest in it "because the automobile is only a novelty — a fad." The lawyer ignored the advice, bought $5,000 worth of stock, and sold it several years later for $12.5 million.

> Lee de Forest, the man who invented the cathode ray tube, said in 1926, "While theoretically television may be feasible, commercially and financially I consider it to be an impossibility, a development of which we need waste little time dreaming."

> Western Union president William Orton rejected Alexander Graham Bell's offer to sell him his struggling telephone company for $100,000. He told Bell, "What use could this company make of an electrical toy?"

> Thomas Watson, chairman of the board of IBM, said in 1943, "I think there is a world market for about five computers."

> Decca Records turned down The Beatles in 1962. An executive said, "We don't think they will do anything in this market. Guitar groups are on the way out."

When railroads first appeared on the scene, the Governor of New York wrote to President Andrew Jackson, "As you well know, Mr. President, railroad carriages are pulled at the enormous speed of 15 mph, by 'engines' which, in addition to endangering life and limb of passengers, roar and snort their way through the countryside, setting fire to the crops, scaring the livestock, and frightening women and children. The Almighty never intended that people should travel at such breakneck speed."

The astronomer Sidney Newcomb wrote in 1903, "Aerial flight is one of that class of problems with which man will never be able to cope." Another well-known astronomer said, "The popular mind often pictures gigantic flying machines speeding across the Atlantic carrying innumerable passengers. It seems safe to say that such ideas must be wholly visionary. Even if a machine could get across with one or two passengers, it would be prohibitive to any but the capitalist who can afford his own yacht."

Fred Smith of Federal Express came up with his revolutionary idea for an overnight air-freight service back in 1965, while he was still a student at Yale. He wrote a paper about it for his economics class. His professor called it impractical and gave him a "C." Six years later Fred launched the company that won him fame and fortune.

Sometimes, of course, the skeptics turn out to be right. Ideas that look brilliant on paper may prove unworkable or too limited in their appeal. But all too often they are rejected for reasons that have nothing to do with their merits. Many people dislike change. They prefer to defend their existing business.

Ironically, some of the strongest resistance sometimes comes from people who have played a major role in previous changes. They not only resent the suggestion that there might be a better way, but have a vested interest in protecting the status quo. One of the most famous examples is Edison's rejection of the argument that alternating electrical current had advantages over direct current. To accept it would have meant that he was wrong and his great rival George Westinghouse was right; it would also have meant that the plant in which Edison's firm already had in operation was obsolete.

If one works for a large and apparently solid corporation it is all too easy to assume that tomorrow will be more or less like today — that significant change is unlikely, unpredictable, and in any case will come slowly. But tomorrow may not be like today; indeed, it is more realistic to assume that it won't be. We live in what has been aptly described as "the age of discontinuity." People everywhere are constantly looking not only for new products but also for new ways of doing things — in manufacturing, in finance, in services, in management, in the arts, in economics. Change is risky, but it may be even more risky not to change.

Henry Ford was one of the business leaders who acknowledged this way back in the 1920s. In *My Life and Work* he wrote:

> If to petrify is success, all one has to do is to humor the lazy side of the mind; but if to grow is success, then one must wake up anew each morning and keep awake all day. I saw great businesses become but the ghost of a name because someone thought they could be managed just as they were always managed, and though the management may have been the most excellent in its day, its excellence consisted in its alertness to its day, and not in slavish following of its yesterdays. Life, as I see it, is not a location but a journey. Even the man who most feels himself "settled" is not settled — he is probably sagging back. Everything is in flux, and was meant to be. We may live at the same number of the street but it is never the same man who lives there.

And later in the same book:

> It could almost be written down as a formula that when a man begins to think that he has at last found his method, he had better begin a most searching examination of himself to see whether some part of his brain has not gone to sleep.

Ford's comments are as pertinent in the 1990s as they were then.

It was another famous American, Andrew Carnegie, who coined the much quoted phrase, "Pioneering don't pay." One can see why. In his day, as now, it could be more profitable to follow others than to lead the way. This is certainly the view taken by many bean-counters. But

Carnegie's subsequent career showed that, in his case, the opposite was true. The fiercely determined little immigrant from Scotland, who started as a bobbin-boy in a cotton factory, became one of the most successful pioneers in the U.S. steel industry, not only in the technological area but also in the organization and management of resources.

Innovation

Carnegie was an innovator, not an inventor. The two terms are often confused. The inventor discovers something new and useful; the innovator takes up an idea and develops it. Many talented people manage to do both, but someone who is good at inventing is not necessarily good at turning a concept into a viable commercial proposition. Many inventors are more interested in the idea as such, and in the challenge it represents, than in the business of making it into a marketable product or service, with all the difficulties and hazards which that involves.

The successful innovator is a *doer* — someone with imagination who can visualize the possibilities of an idea and who has a strong desire to see it realized in concrete form. He or she knows that there will be strong opposition and, very likely, discouraging setbacks. The process may go astray and the results may be disappointing. But there is willingness to have a go and not give up easily. One of the outstanding characteristics of people who have made things happen in this century is their persistence. Ray Kroc, who created the MacDonald's hamburger chain, used to tell his staff:

> Nothing in the world can take the place of persistence. Talent will not; nothing is more common than unsuccessful men with talent. Genius will not; unrewarded genius is almost a proverb. Education will not; the world is full of educated derelicts. Persistence and determination alone are omnipotent.

Kroc is widely credited with inventing the concept of franchising, but this is a myth. It originated in Britain through the brewery/tied public houses system. But Kroc and Colonel Sanders, the man who put Kentucky Fried Chicken on the map, were the first people who recognized the worldwide potential. They did not succeed overnight — it takes a long time to build up an international brand. But they had faith in the concept and the will to make it work.

Individuals like them are often said to be "off their rockers." The accusation rarely bothers them. Jean Paulucci, another entrepreneur who made a vast fortune in the food business, said it was,

> probably the main reason why I have succeeded. I've done things that everybody said couldn't be done, and I've done them in what everybody said was a crazy way. If any young man comes to see and asks how to make his fortune, I tell him to do the same. Don't follow everybody else. Get off the beaten track. Be a little mad.

Innovation tends to be easier for people who run their own business than for managers who work in large corporations. The banks will be cautious, but there are other ways of securing financial backing. It may involve putting your own savings on the line, but you are in charge.

It would be unfair to suggest that large corporations cannot innovate. They can, and do. In some fields they are the only ones who can afford the massive outlay on research and development, or on capital equipment, that is required to convert an idea into profitable reality. But there is no doubt that the bureaucratic structure of some big organizations, and their obsession with short-term results, presents a formidable obstacle to innovation. Employees are expected to follow established procedures; conformity is more highly valued than originality. The individual who attempts to do things differently can easily get into trouble.

This is why many outsiders who try to sell ideas to large firms find it hard to make any headway. The executive who listens to the proposal (if one can find anyone who listens at all) has to weigh up the personal risks involved in supporting it. Do the potential rewards of success outweigh what he or she can lose if the idea fails? It is much safer to say "no" than "yes," and that is what usually happens. The outsider is told that it can't be done because it hasn't been done before, or that "it isn't right for us,"

or because the risks are too great. Sometimes it is adopted at a later stage
— *after* a competitor has made it work so well that the company's position in the marketplace is threatened.

The attitude of senior management is of vital importance. If the chief
executive gives low priority to innovation, little progress will be made. I
am always reminded of what one of the Warner brothers said when the
first talkies came on the Hollywood scene, "Who the hell wants to hear
actors talk?" He soon found out that millions did — it was another
example of lucrative pioneering.

Innovation is about finding new ways of delivering customer value. It
should, ideally, be done in such a way that the company has a competitive advantage which can be protected and sustained. It must be difficult
for rivals to do the same thing for a similar cost.

The Japanese used to be renowned for their skillful imitations. They
also had a knack for spotting opportunities that others had missed. The
founder of Sony, for example, was an obscure inventor who came across
transistor technology on a visit to America. It had been developed by
Bell, but the company did not appear to be aware of its potential. He
saw that it could be used to make radios "small enough so each individual will be able to carry them around for their own use, with power that
will enable civilization to reach even those areas without electricity." So
he got a license from Bell, raised capital, and went into production. It
made Sony a household name far beyond the shores of Japan. Western
companies tend to be more alert these days, and the Japanese have since
put greater emphasis on exploiting ideas of their own, but the story
illustrates what can be done by people with imagination.

Many other innovators have also benefited from travel. Alan
Sainsbury "discovered" the supermarket concept in the U.S. and
imported it to Britain. Anita Roddick, founder of The Body Shop, had
the idea for her business during a year-long trip around the world.
She learned how women in less industrialized societies cleaned and
cared for their skin and hair, and thought that products made from
their natural recipes might also have a market in her own country. She
was right.

Some companies like to buy smaller firms that have pioneered new concepts but lack the capital for expansion. A tempting offer can, in many cases, persuade them to sell. But such acquisitions are seldom much good if the buyer lacks the drive to take the idea to the next stage, or if the bean-counters insist on getting substantial returns before all the building blocks are in place. The founder, who should continue to lead the way, often finds it impossible to work in the new environment and may use the proceeds of the sale to start another business elsewhere.

Innovation is not an isolated event. It is a process that should involve people at every level of the company. The senior management needs to create a *culture* in which it can flourish. Employees must be made to feel that their suggestions and initiatives will be welcomed, not resented. They must expect them to be properly evaluated, but they will give up if every idea is crushed by headquarter committees.

Many large companies are trying to tackle the problem by setting up independent units, or "task forces," which operate outside mainstream management with the maximum possible freedom to carry out specific assignments. IBM created such a force to develop a personal computer to catch up with Apple. Others have followed the example of 3M, which some years ago decided to create new venture teams headed by a "product champion." Each team consists of people with expertise in various areas, including manufacturing and sales. If anyone wants to stop a project aimed at developing a new product, the burden of proof is on the one who wants to stop it, not on the one who proposes it. Paperwork is kept down to a minimum. Failure is forgiven; the senior management wants its teams to keep trying.

The "champion" is the key figure. That person must have all the qualities of a good innovator — imagination, enthusiasm, staying power. The job is to ensure that sound ideas are implemented. To do this, the champion needs the support of an "executive champion" — someone who knows how to deal with the corporate staff, especially the bean-counters. Without this, the champion is unlikely to make much progress.

It also helps if the employers have two separate budgets: an operating budget that covers everything that is already being done, and an innovation budget for new developments. I set up such a system in our own business some time ago.

In magazine publishing, as in everything else, one has to be willing to take risks. Existing titles may fall out of favor or run out of steam. Another publisher may come up with a better idea or new media such as the Internet may mount a serious challenge. You naturally want to maximize your profits on what you already have, but you also know that you must invest in new projects. A separate budget allows you to make a clear distinction.

Our approach is relatively simple. We do our homework and if we decide that the concept has a good chance of success we allocate a specific sum and review the situation after the first year. There may still be a long way to go, but one can generally tell whether it is likely to work or not. If we still think that the concept will succeed we allocate more money. The bean-counters may complain, but happily the decision is not up to them. The managing director and I are putting our judgment and reputation on the line; the buck stops with us. We don't blame failures on others, as so many people in big companies do.

I recognize that the kind of capital we have to commit is small compared with the outlay involved in decisions others may have to make; investment in a magazine is plainly not in the same league as major expenditure on R & D or the building of a new plant. We are not talking about umpteen millions. But the principle is the same. Senior management must give employees the chance to show what they can do, make decisions, and accept responsibility.

A corporate culture that encourages and rewards innovation can reap all kinds of benefits. In its broadest sense, it is about securing real change within an organization, brought about by creative thinking and exchange of information and expertise. New product development is only one aspect; doing things differently is also innovation. I see the process as a spectrum from updating what already exists to producing something completely new; from tweaking something to completely fresh break-throughs.

Pioneering can be painful. It will certainly upset some people. But the notion that it doesn't pay is a myth. Without it, there may be no beans to count.

The Myth of the "Global Marketplace"

PRESSED TO SAY WHERE THEY EXPECT FUTURE GROWTH to come from, many chief executives talk enthusiastically about "the global marketplace." The concept has obvious appeal. There are billions of potential customers out there. A product or service which is successful at home should sell just as well in the rest of the world, right? Well, actually no. As many companies have discovered to their cost, the global marketplace is another myth.

It is important to distinguish between *international* and *global*. "International" refers to cross-border activities between nations, usually bilateral, such as the trade of goods. A "global" market operates across national boundaries as if it were a single market. The difference matters. For a global economy — one marketplace — to work there must be completely free trade among the nations. In reality, there are still all kinds of formidable barriers, even in the European Union.

Theorists have peddled the idea of "globalization" for years. We are all familiar with their arguments. Telecommunications and information technology have changed the world. Trade agreements have reduced protectionism. Capital flows more freely across borders. Television has made it possible to bring products and services to the attention of the masses. Big and powerful corporations operate in many different countries. But ask marketing experts to name a dozen truly global brands. After the usual confident start — IBM, Boeing, Coca-Cola, American

Express, Sony — they soon falter. Virtually all of these were global before the word "globalization" had even entered our vocabulary. Few new ones have entered the pantheon, but such examples give a superficial impression of sameness and have encouraged the assumption that it is easy to develop a "global sell" strategy.

According to a Harvard management guru, Theodore Levitt, "the world's needs and desires have been irrevocably homogenized." This is far from the truth. The fact that we can drive the same car, buy the same soft drink, use the same credit card, and communicate by telephone, fax, or Internet does not necessarily mean that there is now a "global shopping center" where everyone buys the same things.

The theory has proved disastrously wrong for many of the firms which have tried to apply it. The reason is simple: it makes little distinction among the world's regions and cultures. People continue to have different needs and desires. Ask any advertising executive who has had a go at running the same campaign on a worldwide scale.

In all too many cases, the process of "globalization" is product-driven, not consumer-led. The primary aim is to integrate production and make large savings by standardizing product formulation, packaging and sales. There are obvious benefits to be had from such an approach but it is certainly not the whole story.

Consumers, today, have a wider choice than ever before. They do not *have* to stay at the same hotel or use the AMEX credit card to settle their bills. Indeed, there is ample evidence that we are moving in the opposite direction. In advanced economies, customers demand greater individualization and customization and positively shun certain homogenous goods and services. They want diversity, not uniformity.

Think Global, Act Local

American companies have been particularly inclined to fall for the utopian vision of a global marketplace. Many CEOs know very little about other countries. They talk about "Europe" and "Asia" as if these vast parts of the world were identical. Worse, some seem to believe that they are just like the United States. They kid themselves that information networks enable them to "think globally" in the comfort of their office. So they charge into other markets without doing proper homework and are surprised to find that the "global sell" doesn't work.

To be fair, many European companies have made the same mistake about America. It is easy enough to do. Superficially, the United States appears to be one market. Everywhere you look, it seems, there are the same TV commercials and billboards, the same supermarkets and fast-food outlets, the same chain hotels, and the same skyscrapers. There is a single currency and English is the official language. Here again, though, appearances are deceptive. There are significant regional differences which newcomers ignore at their peril.

Some years ago I started a magazine publishing company in New York. I was so confident of success that I bought an apartment in Manhattan. I had a lot of expertise and I spoke the same language. I was, therefore, dismayed to find that ideas that had worked well in Britain did not find ready acceptance in the biggest and most lucrative market in the world. I should have recognized, much earlier, that although there were some prominent national titles they were vastly outnumbered by local publications. New York is not the same as Dallas or Denver. I had visited most parts of the country over the years but I had never really gotten to know them. I employed a team of New Yorkers, but it soon emerged that they had the same shortcomings. I gave up after 18 months. Happily an American company which had its eye on the European market later bought a substantial stake in my London-based core business. It had the good sense not to tell me how to run it — as so often happens in such cases. They recognized that I knew more about publishing in Britain than they did and left me to get on with the job.

This, of course, is the key to most successful overseas operations. Think global, if you like, but act local. Buy a company which knows its market or hire people who can create and develop one for you. Don't put in head office staff who second-guess everything they do and then move back home. Don't send in bean-counters who seek to enforce rigid rules. Don't go on a quick visit and lecture the local managers on what you think they are doing wrong.

It is plainly absurd to imagine that one can deal with China and India in the way as one would do with France or Italy. Yes, everyone likes ice cream. But countries like these are still poles apart, not only because they are at a different stage of development but also because their needs and desires are influenced by different attitudes, tastes and traditions. It is equally absurd to assume that governments will allow their markets to be flooded by foreign imports. The drive towards globalization creates its own resistance.

One of the most obvious barriers to the creation of a global marketplace is that so many governments, particularly those of developing countries, still find it necessary to put up a wide range of daunting obstacles — import duties, quotas, exchange controls, and regulations designed to protect local industries and jobs. Multinational corporations may consider themselves to be immensely powerful and, no doubt, they genuinely believe that they are doing governments a favor by moving into their territory. Surely they have every reason to welcome Western capital and technology? But, as we all know, politicians tend to have their own agenda. In some countries, like Iran, Western products are seen as a corrupting influence. In others, there is a strong sense of national pride combined with a determination not to be pushed around by the multinationals. They may take their money, but they insist that foreign companies must play by their own rules — which can always be changed if it seems politically advantageous to do so.

Even in Britain, which depends so heavily on international trade, we have seen irrational displays of xenophobia. When BMW acquired Rover, for example, there were the usual tawdry comments about the "Krauts" taking over "our heritage." Far from seeing the investment of many millions as a sign of confidence in the country's future, members of parliament and media people worked themselves up into a state of furious indignation. In the United States, there have been equally strident complaints about the Japanese "invasion" and demands for protection. If we can behave like this we should not be surprised if others do the same.

The world's biggest industry, today, is travel and tourism. Most governments promote it, because it brings in foreign exchange (which is often badly needed) and is a labor-intensive business. But it does not command unequivocal support. Many people oppose it because, they say, reckless development is harming the environment and "spoiling" the local population. Coastlines are disfigured; envy of affluent tourists leads to crime; prices go up; traditional ways are abandoned. Economics isn't everything.

Tourism is likely to see continued growth. No sensible government, however, thinks that there is one marketplace for this lucrative trade. When I was chairman of Britain's national tourist organization, the BTA, we were very much aware that each market has different expectations and that marketing campaigns had to be tailored accordingly.

Government controls and local prejudices are not the only obstacles to the globalization of business. For many executives there is another significant problem — a poor command of foreign languages. Americans and the British consider themselves fortunate that English appears to be the language of the global marketplace, but this is not as advantageous as it seems. There are many parts of the world where one really has to speak the local language if one wants to succeed, and even in countries where English is widely used there is considerable scope for confusion.

It is not simply a matter of communication; linguistic skills are also the key to understanding the mentality and culture of people in other countries. They are absolutely vital if one wants to live and work somewhere else. I have seen many executives get into trouble because they assumed that, because the people they were dealing with had a good command of English, both sides were on the same wavelength.

Anglo-Saxons tend to be more direct than Asians. Westerners think that "yes" means agreement when, in Eastern cultures, it may simply be a way to avoid giving offense by saying anything negative or unpleasant. The word "contract" translates easily from language to language, but interpretations vary. To an American, Swiss, German, or British executive it means a binding commitment. But a Japanese may regard it as a starting document to be rewritten and modified as circumstances require. A South American sees it as an ideal which is unlikely to be achieved, but which is signed to avoid argument. We may consider this cheating, but ethics are another issue on which opinions tend to differ. We call the Japanese unethical if they break a contract. They think it is unethical for us to apply the terms of the contract if things have changed. Latinos and many Arabs have flexible views on what is ethical and what is not.

Even people who share the same language sometimes manage to confuse each other. There are marked regional differences in countries like Germany and Italy, and both American and British executives are liable to use expressions which do not indicate properly to the other side what one is really thinking. "Not bad" or "not at all" may sound flattering to an English person, but an American may draw the wrong conclusion. Phrases drawn from sports can be baffling. Americans often use terms from baseball or their version of football, while the British seem fond of cricket analogies like "a sticky wicket" and "a good innings." They tell people that "it's not on" or a "bit thick" and are surprised if others fail to get the message.

Humor has to be used cautiously. It can be a valuable tool for breaking ice, but it can also be counterproductive. In my experience, Germans and the Japanese do not see the point of introducing humor into meetings: business is serious and should be treated as such. Others may find jokes annoying or incomprehensible.

The European Union has 11 official languages. The number of possible linguistic combinations is over 100 and meetings may require more than 30 interpreters. Any move to limit this list to Europe's most widely spoken languages — such as English, German, and French — would lead to a chorus of protests from smaller countries against what they would see as a blow to their national pride and a threat to their culture and traditions. So we have a Tower of Babel, which is set to become even noisier if and when the countries of Eastern Europe are allowed in.

The mental barriers cannot be made to disappear in a hurry, however traditional they may seem. They not only affect consumer choices but also the transfer of knowledge and skills. In theory, it should be easy to move employees around the world. It certainly is an effective way of gaining a better understanding of other cultures, but there is still widespread resistance to such efforts. Even if work permits can be obtained, many managers are reluctant to move abroad. They prefer their domestic environment and want to stay close to where they believe the action is — at head office. The growing emphasis in many countries on services, rather than manufacturing, has created additional problems. It is one thing to apply knowledge and skills in factories; it is quite another to make good use of them in service industries, which tend to be more complex. In many fields, from haircuts to health care, globalization is almost irrelevant. They remain inherently local.

Economists and others have been talking for years about a global capital market as if it already existed. As with most consumer goods, this is not the case. Capital may have become more mobile, and the foreign exchange and money markets may be global, but the conditions for a single capital market have clearly not been met. There should be no financial regulations which restrict its operations in a meaningful way. None of the national participants, including governments, should be in a position to control pricing in the market. All issuers, investors, and financial institutions should have equal access to the same information. All should have a global rather than a national market.

We do not even have a global market in equities. People should, by now, be eager to spread their risks by buying shares in companies all over the world, but relatively few individuals do so. They feel that they don't know enough about foreign markets and companies and don't have the consistent and comparable information needed to make investment decisions. Nor are they sure that government regulations will protect them. So if they think of the world at all, they generally prefer to deal with professionals like unit trust managers. But their record is patchy, because they often underestimate the risks.

In many countries, governments continue to place restrictions on the amount which can be invested offshore, and maintain tight control over the ownership by foreigners of a wide range of enterprises. The curbs will not be lightly abandoned.

Divided Europe

Europe, of course, should have solved these problems long ago. The Treaty of Rome, which established the Common Market, was signed way back in 1957. The aim was admirable: open frontiers, free trade, common laws. Above all it indicated a genuine desire to put an end to the deeply-felt antagonisms which had led to so many wars over the centuries.

There were six original member states — Belgium, France, West Germany, Italy, Luxembourg, and The Netherlands. Britain stayed out, but joined later. Since then we have had the Single European Act and the Maastricht Treaty, both of which committed the membership to a much grander concept — the European Union.

Many people consider it entirely reasonable to assume that we will eventually see a "United States of Europe." Indeed, some of my American friends seem to think that it exists already. There is a European flag, a parliament, a "President," and even an anthem. I am a "citizen of Europe" and have a wine-colored passport to prove it. By the end of the century there should also be a single currency, the euro.

Here again, though, appearances are deceptive. We do *not* have a United States of Europe and I doubt if we ever will. Comparisons with the U.S. are misleading. Europe has a longer history, a much larger population, and a greater variety of customs, languages, and traditions. The concept of federal superstate is a fantasy.

It was not hard to imagine that, one day, six or seven countries might be able to agree on matters like a single currency and a common defense policy. But membership of the club has grown and former communist countries in Eastern and Central Europe, including Russia, are among others who are eager to join. In a few years, Europe is expected to have 26 or 27 members. These nation-states will be wildly different and it seems highly improbable that they can all be welded together in the same way as the U.S.

The Common Market was a relatively simple concept, geared to the needs of business. At the most basic level, it plainly was a good idea to "harmonize" electric plugs. At the broader level, it was equally obvious that business between European countries was more likely to grow if everyone played by the same rules. Much progress has been made in the past 40 years, but it has been slower than the founders envisaged.

Exchange controls have been removed; border controls have been eased; deregulation has begun to bite. Bids and mergers have led to the creation of many more pan-European companies. While politicians have been arguing about issues like national sovereignty, Europeans have quietly forged their own connections. But many barriers remain. Countries like France and Britain, for example, still have quite different legal systems, which can cause problems if one is buying property or a business. The right to live and work anywhere in the Union, which to me is one of the most appealing parts of the club, continues to be challenged in all kinds of ways, especially in countries with a high rate of unemployment. Recognition of professional qualifications is far from automatic.

The variety of languages, and cultural differences, also continue to be a formidable deterrent. There is not much point in setting up a business in the European marketplace if you can't communicate. The rich diversity of cultures is one of Europe's greatest attractions, but it can also be a handicap. Each country has its own newspapers (few of which are read elsewhere) and its own television channels, advertising products which are often totally unknown elsewhere. Labor costs are higher in some countries (and trade unions stronger) than in others. Attitudes toward work, punctuality, corporate governance, and methods of doing business still vary a great deal.

A popular Euro-joke says the ideal employee should have the following qualities, "the internationalism of an Englishman, the charm of a German, the linguistic ability of a Spaniard, the precision of an Italian, the road manners of a Belgian, the generosity of a Dutchperson, the gaiety of a Swiss, the ready wit of a Scandinavian, the sensitivity of a Greek." Unfair, of course, but there is some truth in national stereotypes.

One industry which should, by now, be engaged in widespread cross-border selling is financial services. It hasn't happened. The European Commission has issued more than 50 directives but many have not yet been implemented by member states. There are major disparities between countries, which often amount to blatant protectionism. It is still difficult to mount marketing campaigns which reach out across national boundaries because, in many sectors, there is little consensus on what is acceptable and what is not. Many people have also experienced difficulty in enforcing cross-border contracts. There are other problems which, seen in isolation, may be trivial but which together add up to a significant obstacle. Lack of tax harmonization, for instance, makes it hard to deduct contributions to life insurance or mortgage payments in another state. Documents are not always translated into the language of the consumer or figures are presented in a way which makes people reluctant to do business with a foreign company.

At the macro-level, the next big step is monetary union. The Maastricht Treaty commits European countries to coordinate their economic deficits, prevent excessive policies, and have a single currency. It links the fate of a country's money and capital markets with that of other member states, and affects the internal and external value of the single currency in the same way.

This has several major economic advantages. The first is the range of gains that may be grouped under the heading of "transaction costs." This is not just a matter of avoiding the traveler's commission costs of switching from one money to another at the border; in the bigger scheme of things, these are trivial. Far more important are the risks that fluctuations in exchange rates add to the cost of doing business. The single currency would remove this impediment to the operation of a single market. Advocates of EMU also argue that it would produce increased growth at low inflation.

But there is widespread disagreement about the merits of the scheme. In Britain and some other member states there is passionate opposition to the whole idea, chiefly on the grounds that it would deprive individual countries of their independence. They would no longer be able to manipulate exchange rates, determine fiscal policies, or set interest rates. Given the mess which politicians have so often made of national economies, this may seem like a good thing. But one can see why they are reluctant to hand over control to a central authority. Some also fear that it will hand too much power to Germany, which is likely to be the dominant force in the union.

Some politicians think that Britain should get out of Europe altogether. They choose to forget that, back in the 1970s, a referendum established that we should join the Common Market and that a British government signed both the Single European Act and the Maastricht Treaty because they believed it to be in the national interest to do so. To them, the whole affair has always been a dastardly plot by other European countries to trick us out of our sovereignty and our money. They argue that, instead, we should aim to draw closer to America and to the nations of the Pacific Rim. But this is not a realistic alternative. The European market accounts for half our exports; if we were outside, we would have to pay tariffs on those exports. Inward investment, which has been of such great benefit to Britain's manufacturing and service industries, would decline sharply. The economic consequences would be awful.

Neither America nor Asia has any reason to do us any special favors. The "special relationship," which is supposed to exist between Britain and the U.S. is another business myth, perpetuated by people who cannot accept that the world has changed. Fortunately, both of Britain's main political parties are fully aware of it. They have no intention of leaving the Union; the argument is futile.

If countries like Germany and France remain determined to go ahead with monetary union — and there is every reason to believe that they will — it seems likely to begin in 1999 with at least six member states. There will then be a considerable number of countries that are either unwilling or unable to participate. Britain may or may not join at a later stage. The single currency is a gamble, which could turn out to be one of the best things that ever happened in Europe but which could also be a disaster. It will certainly create confusion.

My own view is that the European Union is likely to be divided into two groups for the foreseeable future. One will aim for political as well as economic integration. The other will seek to establish an association, with different classes of membership. A multi-track, multi-speed, even multi-layered approach will be the pattern as more and more countries apply for membership. We are also likely to see a significant move towards regionalism. It is often forgotten that, for a very long time, Europe was mostly made up of small kingdoms and principalities.

In countries like Germany and Italy, these were not welded together into nations until the last century. The establishment of supra-national institutions has revived old loyalties and ambitions; in a way, Europe is returning to its roots by building again on its regions. They acknowledge the need for unity on issues like defense, but they believe that, in the Europe of the 21st century, it will make sense to strive for autonomy within a wider political framework and to seek partnerships which transcend national allegiances. Regionalism, they insist, is not something which is anachronistic or pure folklore. It is a modern movement and one of progress, which provides people with an identity, a sense of responsibility, and the kind of involvement that fosters enterprise, boosts competitiveness, and acts as a counterbalance to the forces of centralization and intervention which have characterized the development of postwar Europe.

Germany already has a system of government that gives its regions a considerable degree of autonomy, and Britain will probably move in the same direction. Such a development will not make us bad Europeans; on the contrary, it will broaden our vision. There will be no return to medieval times — no frontiers, no fortified cities, no petty tyranny, and certainly not a third world war.

Young people tend to take a more enlightened view than the older generation. Many have traveled extensively around Europe and have forged new friendships. They buy products without worrying about where they come from; they are much more concerned with quality and cost. They eat in Greek and Spanish restaurants; love French cosmetics and Italian fashion; drink Danish beer; collect recordings of English pop groups; and like showing off their German cars. For them, Europe is an adventure full of attractive, interesting people and intriguing new ideas. It is this, as much as anything else, that will shape the Europe of the 21st century. Our cities will become more cosmopolitan; travel will become easier and probably cheaper; there will be a wider choice of financial services as well as products; satellite television and other forms of modern communications will stimulate much greater interest in European literature, music and other arts.

It does not mean that people will abandon their cultural identity or that their needs and desires will be "homogenized." What it does mean is an extension of choice. There will be more competition and, inevitably, more business failures. The companies most likely to succeed are those which recognize that, for the consumer, this extension of choice is the most vital issue.

F·I·F·T·E·E·N

The Myth of the Invincible Dragons

MANY EUROPEANS HAVE A TENDENCY TO SEE THE "Asia Pacific region" as one vast economic community. It leads to other sweeping generalizations. The region is said to be a powerhouse with a common aim: to take over the markets of the world. But, the optimists tell us, its rapidly growing prosperity also offers almost unlimited potential for expansion-minded Western companies.

There is clearly a sizable element of truth in all this. It would certainly be foolish to underrate its capacity to give us a hard time. The Japanese have been doing it for years. But the idea that the Asia Pacific region is a community with shared goals and values is as much of a myth as the notion that there is such a thing as a United Europe or a global marketplace. It takes no account of its geography, history, traditions, cultures and widely different needs.

There are over a hundred different languages and a variety of religions. There are communist regimes in China and Vietnam, and democratic governments in countries like India and Malaysia. Millions of people live in crowded cities; millions more are in villages which have changed little over the centuries. Some work in factories; others toil in rice paddies. There is great poverty but also great wealth. The one outstanding fact about the region, which has more than half the world's population, is its incredible diversity.

Some countries have been rivals or enemies for many generations. Old divisions are not easily set aside; new disputes can flare up at any time.

There are, of course, common interests. Everyone wants more prosperity and access to the markets of America and Europe. Conferences of Apec (Asia Pacific Economic Cooperation) invariably call for the lifting of trade barriers — ours, not theirs. There is more rivalry than unity, with each country competing for a bigger share and resisting demands that it should open its own market to more Western goods and services.

The region has scored heavily in the export of mass-produced consumer goods and raw materials. It will no doubt continue to do so as long as there is an abundance of cheap labor and developed countries do not resort to tough protectionism. In many other fields, however, it is still far behind. It imports more technology than it sells. This is where Western companies are still likely to do well for some time to come — provided that Asian countries are able to pay for it. Many are heavily in debt.

Banks have lent too much money to overextended developers, loss-making state enterprises, and politically connected corporate deadbeats. Fixing this mess could take years and cost hundreds of billions of dollars. This is the darker side of the region's "economic miracle." For decades, Asia thrived amid centralized planning that promoted the accumulation of savings and relied on technocrats to allocate capital efficiently. With competition held down, financial regulators could easily pressure domestic lenders into financing pet projects. The regulators had little regard for profitability. Now the bills for the years of easy credit are coming due.

Japan

Japan is the most important economy by far. Its postwar success in world trade is the main reason why so many people are afraid of what might happen next. But the Japanese are hardly typical. They cannot be categorized as "Asiatics," a Western term which they find offensive. They have a firm belief in the inherent superiority of their race, and are nationalistic to a degree that no amount of politeness can ever disguise.

Other countries in the regions have mixed feelings about them. They are respected and envied but also feared and disliked. Many people will never forgive them for what they did in Asia during the last war. It is highly improbable that history will repeat itself, but one can't blame them for being wary. Many also resent their aggressive behavior in business and accuse them of selfishly protecting their domestic market.

Japan will obviously continue to be a major player, but the 1990s have seen the demolition of another myth: that Japanese businessmen are invincible. The earlier recession in America and Europe, combined with a high yen, had an alarming effect on exports and the "bubble economy" collapsed. Many investments, especially in real estate, turned out to have been an error of judgment. Foreign assets had to be sold, often at substantial discounts, to meet obligations in Japan.

It could be argued that it was simply bad luck, but there was a lot more to it than that. The banks are said to have made so many bad loans that they are in serious trouble; they certainly will find it more difficult to finance entrepreneurial enterprises. Many Japanese have also become more critical of other features of the system — excessive regulation, a bloated and far from efficient bureaucracy, corruption, and the relatively high cost of labor. The concept of lifetime employment is now widely held to be unsustainable. This could lead to a breakdown of the values which have long been regarded as the cornerstone of Japan's success — loyalty, sacrifice, consensus.

On my last visit to Tokyo I talked to a number of employers and executives. They said that change was inevitable. The young were likely to become more independent, more mobile, more in tune with the Western way of life. It was already happening. People were rebelling against *karoshi* — "death by overwork." They wanted to work fewer hours and have more holidays. Similar views have been expressed by Japanese businessmen I know in Britain. They remain patriotic, and they would never dream of being openly disloyal, but they are more open-minded and flexible than they used to be. I am told that Japanese managers in Asian countries still affect an air of superiority, and tend to have an autocratic management style, but perhaps they will also learn that arrogance can be counterproductive.

China and the Chinese

The region's other big player is China. This is the dragon which many people fear will overwhelm us all. The population has grown to more than a billion — a scary number. But the threat has to be kept in perspective.

Despite its efforts to modernize, China is still a largely agrarian society. Two-thirds of the billion are semi-literate peasants who live in small, scattered villages. The country has not nearly reached the levels of industrialization of the former Soviet Union. It has enormous economic and social problems which seem likely to remain the top priority for quite some time to come.

Anyone who has traveled extensively in China, as I have, will be very much aware of the scale of these problems. In many parts it seems that one has stepped back into medieval times. The contrast with cities like Beijing, Shanghai and Guangzhou could hardly be greater.

It is the southern part of this huge country which has seen the most impressive advances and which is displaying the greatest business flair. The addition of Hong Kong makes it, next to Japan, the most formidable competitor in the Asia Pacific region.

America and Europe have played a major role in this achievement. They have contributed badly-needed capital and technology. Western companies have been the driving force behind many important projects. Foreign investment remains a significant factor, but old hands warn against over-enthusiasm. Don't, they say, be seduced by a vision of the potential. China is a big market, but it doesn't mean that newcomers can count on making big profits. The Chinese themselves want to make money by selling to local consumers and they have a head start. Many investments have yet to make the kind of return which companies had hoped for. Many joint ventures have turned out to be disappointing. There is a lot of corruption and, of course, no one knows for sure how the political situation will develop. It is tempting to assume that China will eventually adopt a Western-style democracy, but that seems unlikely to happen in the foreseeable future.

Long-term, the country is more of a threat to its neighbors than to distant Europe and America. I certainly find it hard to believe that its communist regime would ever settle for a helpful role in an Asian Pacific "community." Like Japan, it would much rather be the dominant player.

There is another large group of Chinese — an estimated 51 million — which merits serious consideration. They are the people who have gone overseas, or have been born in other countries. Many live and work in various parts of Asia (such as the Philippines, Indonesia and Malaysia) but they also have established a visible presence in America, Europe and Australia.

Many of us tend to think of them as waiters, chefs, restaurants owners, and small shopkeepers. We love their Chinatowns and crispy duck. But their business interests are much wider than that. They have invested heavily in commercial property, notably hotels and office blocks. In cities like San Francisco, they own a sizable percentage of the real estate. Vancouver has attracted so many Chinese from Hong Kong that wags have renamed it Hongcouver. In New York, Chinatown now includes a large part of which is still called Little Italy.

Britain, too, has many affluent Chinese businessmen. They tend to keep a low profile — unlike some other immigrant groups, they hate to make a public fuss. It is an attitude which has served them well.

In recent years, Hong Kong money has been a significant factor in the London property market. Many wealthy Chinese have bought homes and other property in Britain as a kind of insurance policy. Like the others, they have also armed themselves with Western passports. They want to see what China will do with the former British colony; if things don't work out, they have somewhere else to go.

Their entrepreneurial flair (as well as their cash) makes a useful contribution. Just look at the way Harvey Nichols has been transformed under Chinese ownership. The English might have done better still if we had made them feel more wanted before so many went off to Canada and the United States.

Many overseas Chinese have retained family ties in China. They have no wish to live under communist rule, but have a strong sense of obligation to their relatives. They also know that it pays to maintain and develop commercial links with the country. Their understanding of Chinese culture — especially of the way business is done — gives them a useful advantage. So does their command of English as well as the local language.

Their children, especially those born overseas, tend to take a rather different view. They respect their elders but are more in tune with Western ways. Many have not bothered to learn Chinese and prefer to work for companies outside the Chinatowns. They are accountants, lawyers, doctors, and managers. They live in leafy suburbs and send their own children to local schools. Asia Pacific is an alien world.

Confusion Down Under

Where does Australia fit into it all? It is in the Asia Pacific region, but does not consider itself to be Asian. It still has much stronger cultural ties to the West than to its neighbors. Many Australians maintain that the country's future belongs in Asia, but others adamantly oppose any move in that direction.

Much of the opposition seems to be based on fears that Australia will be "swamped" by Asians. Some people claim that it is already happening, but this is a myth. Asians account for less than five percent of the population. I talked to some of them when I was doing research for my last book, *The Lucky Generation*. They said that they regarded themselves first and foremost as Australians.

Why should it be otherwise? As individuals, they want to make the best life for themselves. Racial conflict is not in their interest, and I expect that they would be just as ready to defend their new homeland, if ever the need should arise, as everyone else. Meantime they have enriched Australian society in many ways. They have brought valuable skills to the country, which is of great help to service industries as well as the manufacturing and agricultural sectors. Like the migrants from Europe, they have played a significant role in making Australia an attractive cosmopolitan society. To a frequent visitor like me, the transformation over the past 30 years has been astonishing — and very pleasing.

The government is more than capable of controlling immigration. The prospect of war is remote. None of its neighbors would dare to contemplate an invasion. The Jeremiahs who say that the country is in danger of being swamped by Asian hordes are talking nonsense.

Australia has many advantages. By geographic chance, it sits on some of the largest reserves of iron ore, bauxite, lead and zinc, nickel, and other minerals in the world. It is a rich country in terms of energy resources, chiefly due to sizable reserves of coal and uranium. The country is also rich in food. Periodic droughts still hamper agriculture, but despite this it has become one of the world's leading producers of beef, veal, mutton and lamb.

Located on the southern periphery of the Asian landmass, Australia is ideally positioned for a thriving relationship with Asia, which is already its largest market by far. If the region continues to develop at the present pace, it stands to reap substantial benefits. It can also expect to see a significant increase in tourism.

Another plus is that the country enjoys a high degree of political stability. Politicians may argue, and governments may come and go, but Australians would never tolerate a dictatorship. There is bureaucracy, but it is not nearly as bad as in most parts of Asia.

All this suggests that Australia is indeed the "lucky country." But, of course, it also has its share of problems. Most of them are homemade. In particular it suffers from relatively poor industrial relations. Strong trade unions have helped to secure Australians one of the highest per capita incomes in the world. They take more holidays than other people, including Americans. They naturally want to keep things just as they are now, but they can hardly ignore what is going on all around them.

Paul Keating, a former Prime Minister, used to blame Australia's ills on years wasted in Anglophilia, torpor, and continuing psychological ties to Britain. It was an exaggeration (Keating was fond of strong language) but his analysis was not without foundation. He argued that the country should become "Asia's odd man in," but denied that it meant it should be Asian in anything other than a broadly geographical sense. What he was trying to say, he explained, is that Australia should aspire to be a truly competitive country that is fully integrated into the economic and geopolitical life of the region. It made a lot of sense to me. His successor, John Howard, has been more cautious but the debate is clearly far from over.

The Myth of the Information Society

THERE ARE STILL NUMEROUS PLACES IN THE WORLD without computers or even telephones. We call them backward but seek them out when we want to get away from it all.

The assumption that everyone shares the same values as us is based on the arrogant belief that our way is best. But as we have seen, there are many different cultures. Some people are quite happy to live without computers, TV, mobile telephones, or fax machines. It is worth bearing in mind when one reads all those articles on the "Wired world" and the "Information society."

Computer buffs naturally want everyone to think that PCs and other electronic equipment are essential to survival. But even in developed countries like Britain and the United States they have a limited role. Someone still has to do all the other things which "society" demands — build homes, fix the plumbing, wait on tables, tend gardens, mind the store, hang wallpaper, bake bread, cook meals, repair appliances, milk cows, grow fruit and vegetables, plow, clean, entertain, and create works of art. The idea that *everything* revolves around information is a myth.

No one would dispute that easy access to information has had a profound impact on business. The telephone has become such an established feature in our lives that it is hard to imagine how earlier generations managed to communicate without it. The history books, of course, tell us how it was done: by carrier pigeon, by hand and smoke signals, and by couriers who often had to travel for weeks through hostile territory. Morse code and the transport of mail by railway came next. The telephone, initially dismissed as a toy, was by far the most significant breakthrough, and others followed. When I started in journalism, in the 1950s, the telex was regarded as a marvelous modern device. Today it is considered as old-fashioned as the manual typewriter. Do you remember the day when, in the early 1980s, you first heard the word "fax" and wondered what, exactly, a fax might be? Millions of other people had the same experience. Today, no business card looks serious without a fax number. The first computer was built in the 1940s and was a cumbersome affair, taking up an entire room. Today's pocket computers can do a better job. Yet even the gadgets which so impress us now will probably look old-fashioned in the next century.

But all this is a means to an end, not an end in itself. The value of information depends on how it is gathered, on its accuracy, and on what use is made of it.

Information — A Mixed Blessing

The basic advantages are obvious. It has simplified and speeded up all kinds of processes, both in manufacturing and services. It is hard to imagine, for example, how airlines and hotel chains would cope without their sophisticated reservation systems. The financial world, too, has been transformed. But there are many areas of business which depend on more than the ability to tap a keyboard and read text and numbers on a screen. Information can help us to form judgments; it is not a substitute for them. It saves time and reduces the element of guesswork, but we still have to make our own decisions. Even the best-informed executive can make mistakes. Good judgment will always be the most valuable attribute.

Many people seem to find it difficult to accept that the information they get may be unreliable. It does not come out of nowhere: someone, somewhere, has had to put it together. That someone may have got the wrong end of the stick, or made use of hearsay, or deliberately set out to mislead. I noted, earlier in this book, how inaccurate statistics can be. There are other pitfalls, including the widespread practice of manipulating information.

Public relations people, for example, often put out press releases which are little more than sales promotion. They can easily create a false impression. Information is slanted, twisted, misrepresented. Achievements may be exaggerated and awkward facts may be suppressed. In politics, "spin doctors" are experts in dissembling. In business too, there are many specialists who have a vested interest in ensuring that everything a company does is presented in a favorable way.

My own profession is not without blame. Journalists frequently print stories which turn out to be inaccurate and TV programs give a distorted picture of what is happening in various parts of the world. It is dangerous to read newspapers casually. That's how the germ of a myth is planted. Next thing you know, it has grown into a fact. A glance at a headline, a swift scan of the introduction, a note of the picture caption, and you are on your way to a firmly held misconception.

I suspect that the main problem for many business people in the years ahead will not be a lack of information but an excess of it. We may drown in data that should be keeping us afloat. Computers should enable people in an organization to do more of what they are getting paid for doing, but all too often it has the opposite effect. An abundance of useless data provides multiple temptations to get off the track, and powerful excuses for doing so.

A report published by Reuters suggests that, although the revolution is said to have barely begun, executives are already suffering from overload. The agency (which, as a major provider, has no reason to be unduly alarmist) called the report, *Dying for Information*. Based on interviews with 1,300 managers worldwide, it said that 40 percent found their work extremely stressful and that two-thirds expected it to get worse as they try to absorb information to keep up with their colleagues and grapple with the potential of the superhighway. The Internet was regarded as particularly damaging because it engenders "information anxiety." People were experiencing "enormous frustration in knowing that the information they need is out there, but that it's going to take them ages to find it."

Managers like these are supposed to be the lucky ones, the élite of the information society, positioned on the inside track in the race for knowledge at the start of a new era. What good will it do their employers if they end up as nervous wrecks?

The truth is that a good deal of the stuff on the vaunted highway is a waste of valuable time unless you are a specialist or a dedicated surfer with nothing better to do. It does not increase our knowledge and it may actually mislead us. It can certainly create confusion.

The Internet was originally developed as a communications network for the Pentagon. It was not designed for doing commerce and no one, at the time, envisaged that it would turn into a monster. Today it is being pulled from all sides: by commercial interests eager to make money on it, by veteran users who want to protect it, by governments who want to control it, by pornographers who want to exploit its freedoms, by parents and teachers who want to make it a safe and useful place for kids. As long as the community was relatively small, it could be self-policing. But now that the population of the Net is larger than most of the countries in the world, those informal rules of behavior are breaking down. Some information is accurate, but there is also much that is bogus, error-ridden or just plain wrong. It has become increasingly difficult to find one's way through it all.

Quality is more important than quantity, which is why many companies employ specialist services or managers who act as filters. Their job is to select what is reliable and genuinely useful. But someone still has to make decisions, which is best done with a clear head.

Many of us continue to be influenced by old-fashioned sources of information — leaks, gossip, confidential briefings, and insights gained over a convivial lunch or dinner with a well-placed contact. A good tip can be worth more than a mountain of data. We also go to conferences, and make business trips, because we recognize the value of meeting people face-to-face. Modern methods of communications may reduce the frequency of such meetings, but they will not replace them for at least two reasons. The first is the need for detailed discussion and explanation, which still requires two or more people sitting down together. You can do it with a video screen, but you will never get that instinctive feel for something which is one of the successful manager's most important assets. The second is the need to establish the rapport which forms the basis of lasting business relationships.

The very effectiveness of the data communications system and the complexity of modern business make it more difficult to convey understanding and more necessary to convey it. This is particularly true of "people businesses" like banking, where so much depends on personal contact and trust. But the same principle applies to other arenas. Trust is hard to build up and easy to destroy.

Information is useful, but you also have to get to know the people you will be dealing with over the months and years. There has to be room for a little gamesmanship, a testing of limits, a chance to access each other's strengths and weaknesses. In a telephone conversation it is often hard to tell whether you have been understood and how your remarks have been received. It is much easier to judge the other person's true intentions when one is working face-to-face.

One should never underrate the social side of business life. It helps to break down barriers and makes it possible to discuss the merits of a proposal in an informal way. Some of the best deals are made, or at least begun, in a bar or restaurant.

There is no doubt that we shall see many more changes in information technology. Some will be of genuine benefit, but not all of it will necessarily mean improvement. It is said, for example, that we shall soon have hundreds of television channels. I don't find it an appealing prospect. Yes, we will have more choice. But if past experience is anything to go by there will be a decline in the standard of programs. When creativity is expected to keep pace with technology it inevitably falls behind.

Can We Trust Market Research?

Many companies set great store by market research. It is a boom industry, because all companies want to know what people think of their products and services. There are many ways of getting information. The foot soldiers, generally, are middle-aged women brandishing clip-boards and button-holing pedestrians in the street to fire questions. Extensive use is also made of "focus groups" of perhaps a dozen people who are encouraged to air their views on a new product or advertisement.

Techniques have improved considerably in recent years. Quantitative market researchers write complex computer models to analyze the figures and to produce a neat set of results. Here again, though, there is scope for error and misrepresentation. Market research is like economics — it tries hard to be a science, but human nature keeps leaving it behind. Customers are asked what they intend to buy, regardless of whether they have given the matter serious thought and often at a time when they couldn't care less. Some make fun of researchers by fibbing. Different focus groups on the same subject may produce utterly different findings. Researchers claim that they know how to cope with the pitfalls, but there have been notable failures. When Coca-Cola decided to launch a "new Coke," for example, it asked 190,000 people to taste it. The result was so favorable that the company went ahead. New Coke, nevertheless, was an embarrassing flop. It was assumed that people bought Coca-Cola just because of the taste. They did not: image is at least as important, and it seems that new Coke just wasn't cool.

In my own field, magazine publishing, faith in market research has also led to expensive disasters. New titles have been launched entirely on the basis of detailed analysis — the interests of social groups, their earnings and spending habits, and so on. Editors were instructed to devise an appropriate product. But a magazine is not just a product: it has to have soul. It must reach out to the reader, engage the emotions as well as intelligence, and provide the reader with insights based on the views and experiences of talented individuals. The editor must have flair and the ability to inspire the magazine's team. If these qualities are lacking, as they so often are, the venture will almost certainly flop.

Some things just cannot be measured. Ask most people how much alcohol they consume, and shame will make them underestimate. Ask others, and they will boast. A third group will not have a clue, because they drank so much that they cannot remember. Income is another tricky one — interviewees may exaggerate to impress, or play it down in case the Internal Revenue is listening.

There is, in my experience, another reason to be wary. Research companies can earn handsome fees by telling clients what they want to hear. It is by no means unusual for reports to be tailored to meet the requirements of executives who will gladly pay for anything which enhances the credibility of a pet project — or destroy one they don't like. It will be an impressive document with lots of numbers, charts, carefully selected quotes, and persuasive jargon. But the conclusions, and recommendations, are more likely to reflect the team's interpretation of the client's needs than an unbiased evaluation of what potential customers have actually said. Armed with this, the executives can go to a management meeting and get the decision they have had in mind all along. It takes integrity and courage to go against the wishes of those who are footing the bill. The better companies will not hesitate to do so, but there are always others who are willing to oblige. Senior managers should be able to see through this. They should certainly insist that the team attends the meeting and answers hard-hitting questions. But many of them simply do not know enough about marketing to be able to form an independent judgment. They assume that the executives have been honest. So it is entirely possible that the wrong decision will be made.

What they say	What it means
This is raw data.	We have an awful lot of stuff, but we haven't worked out what it means. (Have nothing to do with it; insist on a succinct report that indicates the results of the research.)
We believe in scientific decision making.	We believe in finding some statistical basis for the decisions you want to make — and charging you a handsome fee.
We must go into the field.	We must get out of the office and talk to customers.
We recommend in-depth interviews.	We are going to give Joe's mother-in-law a chance to talk for hours.

What they say	**What it means**
We suggest concept testing.	We don't think much of your idea, but we will try to find out how other people feel about it before you go ahead and make a fool of yourself.
On the one hand, on the other hand.	We are not sure what to make of the results, so we have decided to waffle. (Tell them they are paid to come up with firm conclusions.)
Broken down by age and sex.	Not a description of the chairman; simply a way of analyzing answers.
This is based on blind testing.	The products tested have not been identified by their brand because it might influence comparisons and reflect the brand image rather than "pure" product characteristics.
Studies have shown that the degree of correlation between socioeconomic characteristics and consumption is quite small and the practice of using demographics as a basis for deriving media strategies can be challenged.	This research is useless.

Fickle Kings

Some years ago, a U.S. research company interviewed people on their attitude to the Metallic Metals Act — 38 percent said it should be passed. There was no Metallic Metals Act.

In Britain, consumers were shown a list of products made by ICI, which included bicycles. Many people checked this item. ICI does not make bicycles.

These are just two examples of human perversity, exposed by researchers with a sense of humor and the willingness to recognize the shortcomings of their trade.

It is a long-established maxim in business that "the customer is king." Everything revolves around discovering what the customer wants and keeping him happy. But he may not know what he wants until he sees it. (No one asked for a Walkman, for instance.) That is the whole point of advertising. It seeks to *create* a demand.

Agencies naturally claim that they know what will work and that their ads are better than anyone else's. If this were so, clients would not be switching accounts so frequently. The truth is that no one can be sure how people will respond. The head of a major company famously said that, "Only half of my advertising works, but I don't know which half." It was a valid point. For all their research, advertisers can never be certain whether their advertisements sell. The wrong kind can actually reduce sales.

There are obviously times when the customer should *not* get what he wants. He may be eager to get his hands on cocaine, but the law says he cannot have it. He may want accountants to fiddle the books, but reputable firms will rightly refuse to oblige. Many people would even like to see an end to the sale of tobacco.

In the public service sector the notion that the "customer is king" is widely regarded as a joke. Bureaucrats are more inclined to see him as a nuisance. I was once told of an occasion when a talk on customer friendliness was given by the head of a government department. The attendance was surprisingly good. But it turned out that there had been a misunderstanding. The audience thought that the speaker would be talking about the need for customers to be more friendly towards the staff.

There is another myth: that customer loyalty can be bought. The truth is that kings are fickle. They may have favorite brands of soap, or coffee, or detergents, but they seldom buy just one. They tend to have a repertory of four or five and move from one to another. A prime task of advertising is to persuade them to do just that. Many millions are spent on trying to convince them that a product is superior. In some cases, the only superiority lies in the packaging.

Money-off deals and other promotional gimmicks are popular with the sales force, but their effect is ephemeral. Customers will naturally take advantage of them; everyone likes a bargain. Once the campaign has ended, however, they are liable to change to whatever other product appears to offer the same benefits.

The belief that loyalty can be bought is reflected in the proliferation of loyalty schemes. They have worked for *some* companies — British Airways, for example, has gained extra business through Air Miles. Supermarkets have also found loyalty programs useful. It does not follow, however, that they are the answer to every boardroom prayer. They can easily turn out to be expensive exercises with no lasting commercial value, as many companies have discovered.

The effectiveness of loyalty schemes is bound to be reduced if everyone is perceived to be offering something of more or less equal worth. This is exactly what has been happening. Many customers have multiple membership of schemes.

Marketing professionals say that the game allows them to capture a great deal of data. But databases are not much good if they are not put to the right use and if the business provides an inferior service. Sending out an endless stream of junk mail is not enough. This really gets to the heart of the matter: customers will only be loyal if the schemes are backed by more basic elements — product quality, excellent service, value for money. A business that fails in these key aspects is not going to be saved by some fancy scheme. It cannot simply be tacked on to the existing activity; it must be integrated fully with it. You can have the best IT support in the world, but if you can't deliver it isn't worth a dime.

Many of us have in the past tended to be loyal by default rather than choice. This is particularly true of financial services. We simply could not be bothered to switch to another bank, building society, or insurance company. But we have become more promiscuous. As with coffee or detergents, we are much more likely to shop around.

We are also more likely to be swayed by fashion. People who have used a product or service for years will try something else just because it is new or trendy. A restaurant may be all the rage for a while and then find that its customers have changed their allegiance to another establishment — not because the food is any better, but because that's where the "in-crowd" has decided to go next. Film and television producers, designers, pop groups and many others all know how fickle today's customers can be.

A businessman who can't cope with that should find something else to do. There is a nice little story about a grocery clerk, tired of dealing with demanding and often awkward people, who quit to become a traffic policeman. After a few days, a friend asked him how he liked his new job. He said, "The pay and hours aren't too good, but at least the customer is always wrong."

The Myth about Conventions

THE VALUE STILL ATTACHED TO PERSONAL CONTACT, in this electronic age, is reflected in the popularity of conventions. They are an inefficient, time-consuming way of disseminating information and it's a myth that they are held to make decisions. Everything of consequence is usually settled elsewhere.

Most big conventions are Industrial Theater, the equivalent of the vast and boisterous rallies at which the parties allegedly choose presidential candidates. Talking is not enough; there has to be drama. So professionals are hired to put on an impressive show, with rousing music, flashing lights, self-serving videos ("The Romance of Wholesale Plumbing Supplies") and guest appearances by well-known television personalities.

Some conventions may be attended by up to 10,000 delegates. It's a terrifying sight. Ten thousand individuals pushed this way and that, lost in huge assembly halls, the president and other key executives far away on a raised platform, the banquets dreadfully formal and inhibiting.

I find it hard to see the point of such mammoth exercises. Many are little more than an excuse for a binge. People may listen to one or more speeches, if they have to, but most of the time is spent on a golf course or in bars. The challenge, as they see it, is not to find new ways of boosting profits but to get through as much drink as possible. I suppose this is what is meant by the phrase "oiling the wheels of commerce."

Not surprisingly, a kind of convention folklore has emerged among organizers — a collection of tall and untrustworthy anecdotes. They tell of the VIP guest speaker who was unable to deliver a lecture entitled, "Man, Master of the Universe" because the slide projector jammed; the company manufacturing copiers whose joint managing directors turned out to be identical twins; the nationwide chain of discount stores whose conventions always ended with two-and-a-half cheers for the president and the microphone which bent over as Uri Geller collected his thoughts before a banquet speech.

Cynics have defined conventions in a variety of ways:

A convention is a gathering of people who singly can do nothing, but together can decide that nothing can be done.

A convention is an institution for getting people together and telling them what they believe, and why they believe it, while all around them they have the feeling that all the other people who matter believe it too.

A convention is an arrangement that enables people to take a vacation in the company of others whom they see every day of the year.

Conventions are primarily a means of enabling people with some common interests to present a united front against the outside world.

The last one probably comes closest to the truth. The annual conferences of large companies are, above all, a mass affirmation of the credo that the corporation is a wondrous entity, and that higher sales and profits are the most important things on earth. IBM even used to have its own songs. The management is now rather shameful about them, and they are rarely heard, but a brief extract from one will give you the flavor:

March on with IBM. We lead the way!

Onward we'll ever go, in strong array

Our thousands to the fore, nothing can stem

Our march forever more, with IBM.

March on with IBM. Work hand in hand,

Stout-hearted men go forth, in every land

Our flags on every shore, we march with them

On high forever more, for IBM.

Some of the stout-hearted men (women, presumably, didn't count in those days) must have found it hard to remain serious.

Trade associations, councils, chambers of commerce, and assorted federations all run conventions because it is expected of them. They are supposed to enhance their status and bring in new members. They certainly boost the egos of their officers and others who may be invited to speak. Like the delegates at party conventions, they can fool themselves that the people in power are influenced by their views. Resolutions are passed and statements released to the press, which rarely pays much attention to them.

Convention man is a strange creature. He may strike you as a perfectly sensible, down-to-earth fellow when you meet him over lunch or a drink. His language is blunt and direct. But when he ascends a platform he is liable to become a pompous bore. Convention Man calls on governments to build a "New Tomorrow, Face the Future, Cut Red Tape, Reward Enterprise, Meet the Challenges" ahead. He has heard politicians use the same platitudes, and he knows that they are safe. No one is going to disagree with a view everyone shares. Who doesn't want to build a better tomorrow? Who is in favor of red tape?

Many business types manage to sail through numerous conventions by using a simple recipe. Take half a dozen quotes from long-forgotten political speeches, add a few generalizations, stir in a few jokes and flattering comments about the host and the audience, and serve in a breezy manner. If they are addressing people from their own company, they congratulate everyone on their achievements, thank the spouses for their support, mention the vital need for profits, and urge them to try harder still.

The chairman or president may get away with it — he is listened to with respect even when he is talking the most awful rubbish. Others cannot count on the same treatment, and there is no reason why they should be able to do so.

International conventions are often the most dangerous of all, because of the difference in culture as well as languages. You may give offense without knowing it, and a translator may convey a garbled version of what you have said.

You are reasonably safe if you sing the praises of freedom, brotherhood, and friendship. Take this splendid remark made by Stalin (of all people) in 1952, "The peaceful co-existence of capitalism and communism is fully possible given the mutual desire to cooperate, readiness to perform obligations which have been assumed, observance of the principle of equality and non-interference in the internal affairs of other states." What could be nicer? Well, perhaps this sentence or two from the communiqué put out at the end of one of those pretentious summits which world leaders are so fond of. The convention agreed that:

> Internal economic policies designed to curb inflation and rises in the cost of living should be steadily followed. Sound economic development should be encouraged with the object of increasing productive strength and competitive power, providing employment, and raising the standard of life.

Smaller conferences tend to be more worthwhile. People from different branches or divisions have chance to get to know each other better, and to exchange ideas and information in a meaningful way. There is generally much less grandstanding. Break-out sessions can address specific problems. The chief executive can spell out his vision — if he has one. But most of this could be achieved in other ways, which is why some companies have started to question the value of these tribal powwows. There is no easy answer, because it is virtually impossible to measure the benefits.

Making a Speech

This kind of waffle will clearly not work if you are asked to speak at a high-level conference of fellow executives on some specific topic. The organizers may also ask you to produce a paper. If you settle for platitudes, you will inevitably be regarded as someone who has nothing worthwhile to contribute. The audience will be appalled by your lack of depth. Your reputation will suffer.

This is obviously true of medical conferences and other professional gatherings, which tend to be serious in purpose and execution. I once found myself at a convention of the Modern Language Association in New York. Almost all the delegates were Ph.D.s and the papers had daunting titles like, "The Semantic Features of the Machismo Ethic in English" and the "Cunning Spontaneities of Romanticism." I kept my mouth firmly shut. But business conferences, too, sometimes have a more ambitious aim and any speaker who tries to make do with empty phrases will end up feeling foolish.

The main lesson I have learned from these occasions is that it pays to stick to the topics one knows best. It may seem obvious, but it's surprising how many people chance their luck in areas they know no better than anyone else. You are much more likely to impress an audience if you specialize. Your experience and knowledge of the subject will come through, and you will be able to challenge conventional thinking without making people angry. You will also be able to work in some neat little plugs for your own triumphs and pet schemes.

To do this, of course, you should try to get as much information as possible about the aims and framework of the conference, and about the kind of people who are expected to attend. Insist on certain details, no matter how hard-pressed the organizers may be. There is a world of difference between addressing 50 people and 500, or between an audience of fellow experts and one of laymen. What is the rest of the program, and how do you relate to it? What does the program committee hope to accomplish? Who will be there? Will there be questions afterwards?

The pitfalls are legion. Committees have a penchant for thinking up smart but misleading titles. Or they will be deliberately vague because no one has ever actually decided what the conference is about. Some years ago I toured a number of American cities on behalf of one of the country's biggest stockbroking firms. My brief was to talk about Europe's financial and economic problems. In St. Louis, Chicago, and San Francisco the audience was small, businesslike, obviously well-informed and attentive. When I got to Los Angeles, my sponsors urged me to make exactly the same speech. But when I arrived at the venue the ballroom of the huge Century Plaza Hotel — my heart sank. Six hundred smartly dressed people, professionals and their spouses, were drinking heavily and watching a group of dancers who had been specially flown over from Hawaii for the evening. A brief chat with two or three of the guests confirmed my opinion that no one gave a fig for the financial problems of Europe; they were there to have good time. I found the Organizing Secretary and remonstrated. "Oh," he said, "we knew that. But you go ahead as planned. We are paying the bill — and it mustn't be all enjoyment." I went into the foyer, sat down in a comfortable chair, and considered my position. I obviously couldn't walk out. But I also knew it would be disastrous if I delivered the speech I had in my pocket.

Fortunately, Mr. Orben came to the rescue. Orben was a clever fellow in New York with a talent for composing topical one-line jokes. A friend had given me one of his comedy guides a few days earlier and I hastily worked a dozen or so of the best gags into my script. Half of them, I recall, were about General de Gaulle, then highly unpopular because of his attacks on the dollar. Two or three were about the poor old pound. I was tempted to include some about California, but decided against it because Americans do not, as a rule, like to hear foreigners joking about their habits and institutions. Like the British, they prefer to laugh at others rather than themselves. Thus armed, I mounted the rostrum. The audience looked dismayed when the chairman announced the title of my speech. I struggled on until I came to my first joke. It brought the house down. Bolder now, I talked a bit more about Europe and then told the next one. And so on. The evening was saved.

Ever since I have taken good care to ask searching questions before undertaking to speak anywhere. And I have not hesitated to change my speech to suit the mood of the occasion.

A word, though, about jokes. Remember that we live in an age of "political correctness." Never tell one which may be regarded as sexist or racist. It isn't always easy to resist the temptation, because some audiences love them. When the platitudes are done, even chief executives are wont to sip bourbon, nudge each other, and tell the one about the actress and the bishop. I realize that, whenever I face an after-dinner audience, that they expect to hear another dreary recital of platitudes and long for some new spicy jokes. They would be annoyed if anyone had the bad taste to tell one over a business deal, but the evening is supposed to be different. The timid and polite are usually embarrassed by them (and rightly so) and top executives tend to be filled with remorse when they wake up the next morning. Some carefully built reputations have taken a dive after 8 P.M.

There is no reason why a good doctor, engineer, accountant, or textile manufacturer should also be a good speaker. It takes training and practice to do well. Many people lie awake half the night in a strange bed somewhere in a strange town, terrified of the "ordeal" which awaits them the next day. They fervently wish they had stayed at home. When it's time to speak they apologize for their inadequacy, stumble through sentences in which they have no confidence, forget the punchline of their jokes, and generally have a thoroughly miserable time. But that could never happen to you, could it?

The Myth that Success Will Set You Free

SUCCESSFUL BUSINESS PEOPLE ARE MUCH ENVIED. We tend to assume that, having made a large fortune, they are free from worry. This is a myth.

In theory the rich should be able to lead a life of ease. They can devote the rest of their day to the pursuit of pleasure. Some do just that, but many continue to work hard — and worry — long after they have made more money than they can ever hope to spend. It is a curious phenomenon.

Greed is one explanation. For some the accumulation of more and more money is an end in itself. But greed is not the only driving force. People from humble backgrounds often harbor a deep-seated feeling of insecurity, dating back to childhood, which they cannot shake off. They keep going because they are afraid that fate may rob them of their wealth. Others are workaholics who don't know how to stop. They have no outside interests and fear that they may get bored if they retire. But many are in love with power and the thrill of the chase — the kicks to be had from outsmarting rivals and doing deals. For them money as such has ceased to be important; it is merely a way of keeping the score. They are gamblers who get turned on by big risks. Worry is part of the game. Deals may go wrong, but they are exciting.

Some get into trouble with the law. This is what happened to Ivan Boesky, one of the most famous players on Wall Street in the early

1980's. Boesky was an expert in the financial game known as " risk arbitrage." He did not invent it, but he was the first to set up a business devoted purely to arbitrage and the first to bring investors into his operation — pioneering efforts which, because he was so successful, impressed both Wall Street and the media. He risked vast sums and made staggering gains: by 1986 he was reckoned to be worth $280 million. It would have been a good time to quit, but he resisted whatever temptation he might have felt to do so. He still started work at 7 A.M. and spent the whole day — often until midnight — making deals.

Investors were constantly reminded of the phenomenal returns from buying takeover stocks before the takeovers were publicly known. *Business Week* dubbed him the " Pied Piper of Arbitrage," and financial journalists wrote admiringly about his legendary list of contacts. The Securities and Exchange Commission, though, was not so easy to impress. It started an investigation into his methods and eventually charged him with insider trading. Others were subsequently accused of the same crime, but Boesky's case got the most publicity because of the scale of his deals. The tip-offs to the SEC that were his undoing came from another trader, who hoped that it would secure him more lenient treatment. Once charged, Boesky himself agreed to cooperate in the government's continued probe of insider rings. He was nevertheless ordered to pay a fine of $100 million and was sent to jail, where he had ample time to reflect on his folly.

Many other self-made millionaires, and even billionaires, are prisoners of the business they run. They believe that, if they let up, it will fall apart. It is the same kind of vanity that drives on so many of the alleged corporate supermen. If they have a controlling share at stake it is usually impossible to dislodge them.

The charitable view is that they have a strong sense of responsibility to the company. This may well be true, but some would serve it better by standing aside and letting someone else have a go.

Such people often boast that they never take a break. Vacations are for wimps. They seldom count the cost in terms of health, personal relationships, and peace of mind. They appear to be indifferent to the misery it may cause their families. If their spouses complain they can always find others. Their new partners may turn out to be gold-diggers, but so what? The world will be impressed by their latest glamorous acquisition. Few of their acolytes have the courage to point out that, far from being impressed, the world will probably be amused by their delusions.

Only one thing is liable to stop them in their tracks: sudden, unexpected illness. Many find it hard to come to terms with it. They are so used to controlling every aspect of their lives that they tend to take good health for granted. ("I don't have ulcers, I give them," the late movie mogul Harry Cohn famously told an interviewer). God gave them talents denied to others; surely He isn't going to take it all away, while allowing ignorant peasants to enjoy glowing health right into old age? He can, and he does.

This is the point at which the rich usually start to ask themselves the obvious question: what has it all been *for*? Did they really need more millions? Should they have stepped down earlier and taken up a hobby? If the illness is scary, like cancer, they may do just that if they are lucky enough to survive. But if it is easily cured, they may not heed the warning; once out of hospital they go on as before.

Benjamin Franklin once said that, "success has ruined many a man." He was right.

The Myth of the Lucky Kids

Many rich people have another reason for their relentless quest: they want to create a dynasty. A common argument is that " I want my children to have a good start in life." Nothing wrong with that, of course, but it often disguises the real motive. They don't want their offspring to enjoy themselves, but to follow their example.

The children of the rich are widely thought to be lucky. They don't face the same financial struggles as those from poor families. An accident of birth has given them everything they could wish for. Or so it seems. In reality, the idea that having rich parents guarantees happiness is a myth.

Many of them lead confused and often unhappy lives. Some are emotionally insecure, because their parents have been too busy to show them the kind of love which every child needs, and because they are terrified that they will be unable to live up to the high expectations placed upon them. Others resent the notion that they are mere appendages, a part of the parental ego trip. They hate the assumption that they are there to play whatever role is assigned to them. They feel that they are being taken for granted, that they are deprived of choice, that their path has been mapped out without anyone ever bothering to ask what *they* want to do. They are bullied by their successful parents, envied by their friends, resented by self-appointed critics, and exploited by ruthless opportunists. Some become alcoholics or drug addicts.

If such children join the family business, as many of them do, they have to cope with prejudice. It will be widely assumed that they have managed to secure their job because of the position held by their parents, not because they possess any merit themselves. They will be courted, in the hope that the flatterers may be able to hitch a ride, but they will find it hard to earn respect.

What many rich children want, above all, is a real sense of personal worth: the feeling that they matter *despite* their privileged background. It may be impossible to achieve within the family firm, which is why they so often seek jobs with other companies even if it means having to perform lowly routine tasks. They long to be treated just like everyone else, and they go out of their way to achieve that objective. Some try to make their mark in other fields — the theater, painting, publishing, sports, and so on. They may back their resolve with an open denunciation of wealth and the habits of the rich. It is not unusual for them to become involved in causes which set them in direct opposition to the financial interests of their parents or other relatives.

Such opposition, not surprisingly, can become a major cause of friction. The parents see it as an act of betrayal or, at the very least, as an appalling display of ingratitude. Wise parents recognize that most young people go through an idealistic phase and refuse to be goaded; they reckon that there is a good chance that, in time, kids will curb their rebellious instincts. But often the friction turns into a fire: the angry parent may decide that, if the child is so firmly against all that the family believes in, and all that the parents worked so hard to achieve, they might as well stop the child's allowance, or even disinherit him or her. Unfortunately for parents like this, this response has become much more difficult. The creation of trust funds and other instruments designed to avoid tax and maintain control of the business has given the children of the rich a greater degree of independence than they have ever had before.

I have always been fascinated by what happened to the late Paul Getty, once the richest man in the world. Getty had five sons and he thought that, if he concentrated on building up a big business empire, everything would fall into place. He was wrong.

At one time or another, each of the four older boys tried his hand in the family business. Two dropped out after relatively brief periods. Ronald went into the movie industry; Gordon chose to follow artistic and intellectual pursuits. Eugene Paul showed early promise (to please his father, he even changed his name to Paul Getty, Jr.) but lost interest after a spell with Getty Oil Italiana and left. Timothy, the youngest, never got the chance to try; he died at the age of 12, after undergoing several operations for a brain tumor. George, the eldest, was the only one who looked like a potential successor and was, accordingly, groomed to take over.

As a child, George saw very little of his father. (Even at the age of 33, when he had three daughters of his own, he reckoned that he had spent no more than six weeks with his own father since he was one year old.)

George served in the army and then went to Princeton University. His aim, at that point, was to become a lawyer. But when he left Princeton he announced that he had changed his mind: he would go into the oil business. Paul was delighted and promotion was swift. George became president of Tidewater Oil, one of the principal companies, and heir apparent to the emperor's throne. By all accounts, he did a competent job. But Paul denied him effective control: he had to consult his father before he could make any decision. Convinced that he could never win however hard he tried to please, George began to drink heavily and took medication in order to sleep. His marriage deteriorated. One evening in

1973, Paul was called at a dinner party and told that his eldest son was dead.

At first he was led to believe that George had suffered a stroke, but the next day an autopsy revealed that the cause of death was an overdose of barbiturates and alcohol. He ordered an independent investigation and was told what he wanted to hear: that it was an unfortunate accident. But he could not shake off one nagging question; was it possible that the pressures for George were greater than for other business executives because he strove too hard to emulate his father? He later said that he had learned an important lesson: you cannot predetermine your children's careers or the course of their lives.

I can honestly say that I have never attempted to do so myself. I tried to guide my children to the best of my ability when they were young, but I did not force them to do anything they did not want to do. I offered advice and help when it was sought, and still do, but I have always held the strong belief that we should all do our own thing.

The Myth that Tips Will Make You Rich

ONCE AN INDEPENDENT COMPANY HAS REACHED a certain size, and obtained a stock market quote, it will be closely watched by another group of "experts" — fund managers and investment advisers. Stockbrokers, unit trusts, pension funds, banks and many others all have people who claim to know much more about the market than the rest of us. The obvious question is why, if they are so good at it, they work for a living. It would surely be far easier to trade on their own account, as angels do. The short answer is that most of them are not as good as they would like us to think they are. The popular notion that Wall Street has financial geniuses by the hundreds is an enduring myth.

Many outfits, to be sure, employ managers and analysts with impressive academic credentials and years of responsible service. Standards have risen considerably since I worked for a firm of stockbrokers in the early 1950s, and regulatory controls have been tightened. Information is easier to come by and generally more reliable. Analysts keep in touch with business trends, examine annual reports with considerable care, and talk to the heads of companies. They know the tricks that can be played with numbers. But it should not be assumed that they are better at making judgments than others, or that they are doing all this on behalf of small investors. That would be far from the truth.

Many advisers stress the word "professional" when describing themselves. They are right, of course. A professional is someone who works for money, as against the amateur who does it for other reasons. But don't think that a "professional investment adviser" is automatically more than the dictionary says he is. Some are little more than salesmen, motivated by commission. My bank has an "adviser" who regularly calls to tell me about the great investment opportunities he has discovered. Some make sense; others do not. His expertise appears to lie largely in persuading people to buy what he wants to sell. The same is true of many others in today's highly competitive field of financial services. The plain fact is that the directors of financial institutions are far more concerned with what their company gets out of each transaction than with what is appropriate for you.

None, of course, would survive for long if they consistently mismanaged the funds entrusted to them. Their "experts" try hard to beat the market averages. Some succeed; others get it wrong more often than they care to admit.

Most advisers agree that successful investment requires selectivity and timing: buying the right stocks at the right price and selling them when their potential wanes. But within this broad agreement, almost unlimited differences of opinion exist over how to combine these components into an investment program. The differences are reflected in the range of investment services and their approaches.

Tipsters

I was a share tipster myself, for a time, as financial editor of one of the Sunday newspapers. Readers expected me to tell them, each week, how they could make a quick capital gain through speculation. I did my best, but I was very much aware that there is a considerable element of hit-or-miss about it all. The late Bernard Baruch, who was regarded as one of the wisest men on Wall Street in his day, once said that if a speculator was correct half the time he was hitting a good average. I though it was a valid point; I still do.

Then, as now, the stock market was awash with rumors which rarely had any substance. I was invited to lunch with chairmen and CEOs who talked enthusiastically about their business, in the hope that I would give them a favorable mention in my column. Stockbrokers sent me circulars which listed their own recommendations, a move that was equally self-serving. I also met people who insisted that they had inside information. It nearly always proved to be false. Today, of course, you may be jailed if you act on genuine insider information.

A leading businessman once offered me an attractive deal — he would put up a large amount of money and I would gamble with it, losses to be taken care of by him and profits to be shared. It wasn't hard to say no, because I would not have remained a city editor for long if I had agreed.

My boss at the time, the late Lord Beaverbrook, insisted that his financial journalists should stay out of the market. He felt that we would be tempted to exploit our position. Some of my colleagues on other newspapers took a different view. They argued that tipsters had as much right to make money as other professional advisers; a stockbroker would not hesitate to buy the shares he had recommended and no one would think it wrong for him to do so. A tipster who followed his own advice, moreover, would be more likely to understand the thinking — and emotions — of his readers than someone who saw the whole business as an abstract exercise.

I thought this was humbug and still do. A financial journalist who speculates has a distinct advantage; he can tip a share, watch it go up as readers act on his advice, and then unload them at a quick profit without telling anyone that he has done so. He is indeed abusing his position.

The tipster may face other pressures. I once worked on a newspaper whose editor was an enthusiastic speculator — so much so that the city editor felt compelled to keep a watching brief on his portfolio. Four or five times a day he would shout "score-sheet," and an assistant would dash into his office with the latest price movements. Harmless, perhaps, but how could anyone be sure that it did not influence the financial editor's judgment?

There are, today, some 14 major tipsheets in Britain alone, with circulations ranging from 5,000 to 25,000. Sales figures are sketchy, even though it is important to know how widely the information is spread.

Read any advertisement by the "I gotta share" people and you would think that you were on the automatic road to riches. They all boast winners, often with astronomical returns, but they often fail to tell the whole story. Many take the "scatter gun" approach. They mention scores of shares, taking the credit for those that go up while ignoring the rest.

Between them, these tipsheets issue more than 3,000 different buy recommendations a year. TipTracker, a research company which buys all the sheets and analyzes them, reckons their record is mixed. In 1996 only five did better on average than the gain in the FT All-Share index. The worst would have lost investors more than five percent of their money.

The Internet has created new opportunities for tipsters. A burgeoning number of sites are targeted at the small investor. Most are simply online discount brokerages, conduits to conventional investment firms, but some are also used by unscrupulous people to inflate stock prices through sheer hype. They tend to concentrate on super-volatile high-tech stocks, and although sites usually include disclaimers, many greedy speculators are seduced by the hucksters.

On Wall Street, all kinds of absurd theories have been aired in the past to support "buy" recommendations. Some tipsters have claimed to be able to predict what would happen to the market by studying sunspots, analyzing dreams, and using mass telepathy. I even met a man once who claimed that stock prices share something with the mouse population of a 20-acre field in central New York State. Both, he said, were governed by cycles. I was too stunned to ask him how he kept count, but I suppose his theory was no more idiotic than the one advanced by another New York investment adviser who said his information came from a daily newspaper comic strip. Each strip, he maintained, contained a market code. If, for example, the main character's right hand was in his pocket, the hidden signal meant "buy." If two puffs of smoke rose from his cigar, it meant that the second hour of trading would be especially strong. The adviser was eventually brought to court on a charge of misrepresentation and, not surprisingly, found guilty. The judge must have found it hard not to laugh.

Britain, of course, has also seen some bizarre demonstrations of the gullibility of speculators. Indeed, we got there ahead of the Americans. The first great stock market speculation, early in the 18th century, centered around the South Sea Company, which had been granted a British government franchise to explore South America and the Pacific. It had no other assets, but its first public share offering met with an enthusiastic response. Other companies were hastily formed to cash in on the general mood of optimism. Many had preposterous objectives such as "importing a large number of jackasses from Spain." One promoter announced, simply, that he was forming a company "for an undertaking which shall in due time be revealed." Everyone got in on the act and London's Exchange Alley was blocked day after day by crowds eager to buy stock. In the words of a ballad published at the time:

Then stars and garters did appear

Among the meaner rabble;

to buy and sell, to see and hear

The Jews and Gentiles squabble.

The greatest ladies thither came,

and plied in chariots daily,

or pawned their jewels for a sum

to venture in the Alley.

The tipsters had a marvelous time: speculators were ready to believe in anything they were told, no matter how outrageous it might be. The bubble burst when the South Sea Company suddenly collapsed.

The 20th century has seen many other examples of speculative excess. The most famous was the boom that led to the great stock market crash 1929. It ruined countless people. In the 1960s there was a new issues mania that rivaled the South Sea Bubble in its intensity. It was called the "tronics boom," because the stock offerings frequently included some garbled version of the word "electronics" in their title even if the companies had nothing to do with the electronics industry. Buyers didn't really care what the companies made, so long as it sounded electronic. Many prospectuses carried a strong warning. "This company," they said, "has no assets or earnings and will be unable to pay dividends in the foreseeable future. The shares are highly risky." But no one can prevent a speculator from acting foolishly if he is determined to do so. The tronic boom ended in 1962 with a horrendous selling wave.

During the 1980s another speculative mania came into being. This time the emphasis was on the new fields of biotechnology and micro-electronics. Fifteen billion dollars worth of stock were floated within a few months. As before, everyone wanted to get in on the act. As before, the bubble burst. By the end of the decade, most biotechnological stocks had lost three-quarters of its market value.

One would like to think that people have become more sophisticated — that they recognize the dangers of what Alan Greenspan, the chairman of the Federal Reserve, has called "irrational exuberance." But I wouldn't care to bet on it.

Many professionals firmly believe that analyzing the behavior of the crowd, and trying to anticipate what it will do in future, is more profitable than basing decisions on the intrinsic value of stocks. This is known as the "castle-in-the-air" theory of investing and past experience clearly indicates that it has merit. Forget logic; all that counts is mass psychology. There is a sucker born every minute — and exists to buy your investments at a higher price than you paid for them.

The Importance of Timing

As a financial editor, I considered it to be part of my job to criticize companies, when necessary, and to speak up when I thought it was time to sell a particular stock. This was unpopular. Readers wrote to complain that I was "damaging" their investment. In my replies, I often quoted the great Nathan Rothschild, who said that he had made his fortune by always selling too soon. His formula was "sell, regret — and grow rich."

Many amateurs don't seem to understand the importance of timing. Until one sells, a paper profit is just that. It may evaporate if one hangs on too long. It is irritating to get out and then see the price go up, but it is even more irritating to stay in and watch it dropping like a stone. When that happens, the amateur tends to find it hard to accept that he may have made a mistake. He cares too much about the price he has paid; if he shows a loss he frequently sits tight in the hope that sooner or later the shares will get back to their old level. Sometimes they never do. By cutting his loss, and reinvesting in a more promising stock, he could have done better. The golden rule is to ask yourself whether the original reasons for buying are still valid. If not, sell. Don't invent other reasons for holding on.

Some financial advisers prefer to talk about the market, rather than individual shares, and to stick to generalizations which sound good but don't mean a thing. They will tell you that the market is likely to "move sideways" or that "it is bound to fluctuate during the coming months." They trot out old clichés like, "a stock is worth what people will pay for it" and urge you to watch out for opportunities to "pick up bargains," or to be "highly selective," without actually telling you where the bargains are or what to select. Stockbrokers, who are very much aware that such a half-hearted approach doesn't create business, tend to be more decisive. But even they often come up with losers.

Financial genius is a rising stock market. You don't have to be an expert to do well when everything is going up. The real test is how you get on when it starts to move in the opposite direction. Professionals are supposed to be good at spotting major turning points, but often miss the boat. A downturn may be described as a "temporary correction"; the market can drop a great deal before they concede that more than a correction is happening.

Bull markets traditionally end in a speculative frenzy, with the public bidding up prices of fourth-rate companies and paying premium prices for hitherto unknown firms that have just gone public. Floating a business is one of the major activities of investment bankers and brokers, but their advice is more likely to be of benefit to the people who are doing the floating, and to fund managers, than to the small investor.

Even professionals can get caught. One of the most extraordinary episodes of the early 1980s was the boom in junk bonds — unsecured, high-interest securities which received low ratings from credit-rating agencies (hence the term junk). The pioneer of this bizarre version of the money game was Michael Milken, who managed to persuade many of the big institutions in the U.S. that they were less risky than they had thought. The bonds were widely used to finance hostile take-over bids and in 1985 alone more than $18 billion's worth were issued. They did absolutely nothing for the economy and proved to be disappointing investments. In 1989 Milken and his brother Lowell were indicted on 98 counts of racketeering and securities fraud; in 1990, Milken was given ten years in prison.

Financial Games

The amateur usually has private affairs to see to and limited time and attention to give to the ins and outs of the stock market. He may prefer to leave investment strategy to his broker or to the people who run mutual funds. The growth in the popularity of mutual funds during the past few decades is another remarkable development.

The concept can be traced back to Britain in the late 1860s; an early exponent was a Scottish textile executive named Robert Fleming, grandfather of the man who invented James Bond. Its most consistent attraction has always been that, by putting up a relatively small sum, an investor can participate in the advantages of a large, diversified and well-managed block of investments. It is a sensible approach, and many people have benefited from it. But there is no guarantee of success and the investor has to pay for the privilege of having his money looked after by someone else.

When mutual funds began to make a significant impact on the European public in the early 1960s, there were some dubious ventures. The worst example was the company launched by Bernie Cornfeld, called Investors Overseas Services. Cornfeld had started as a salesman for an American mutual fund. But business in New York was tough and he decided to try his luck in Europe. Arriving in Paris in 1955 with a few hundred dollars in his wallet he soon saw the possibilities of a large expatriate market,

especially American servicemen. He decided to become an independent dealer and persuaded other Americans living in Paris at the time to help him. In 1958, he moved the base of his growing sales force to Geneva and later launched his own mutual funds. He devised an advertising slogan, "Do you sincerely want to be rich?" His salesmen loved it. He also hit on what many of them thought was a brilliant idea: a "Fund of Funds." The aim, he explained, was to reduce the risk still further by investing in other mutual funds. The ordinary man would have professionals choosing the professionals who made the decisions. What could be safer? It meant paying two management fees, but most of his customers did not seem to mind. He then had another stroke of inspiration: why not reorganize things so that IOS could collect both fees? All that it required was that the company itself should control the funds into which the money went.

The sales force combed the whole world for people's savings and his managers put them into funds which IOS ran. But the products had one basic flaw. In the long run one's sales have to be matched by performance, and Cornfeld failed to do so. The whole edifice eventually collapsed because the money was so badly managed. When the world's stock markets went into a sharp decline, the value of his dizzy speculations plummeted and many investments were wiped out altogether. No one wanted to buy his fund shares any more; hordes of investors, painfully aware that his promises could not be kept, deserted him.

IOS was, first and last, an organization run by salesmen for salesmen. It was they who profited most from the vast flow of money which the company handled. His financial counselors did not have to be investment experts; Cornfeld told them that after one week's sales training they would be able to go out and sell mutual funds to strangers anywhere on earth. He gave them a text cast in the form of a dialogue between salesman and prospect, which they were supposed to learn by heart.

"Mr. Geldt," it began, "let's presume that you had $1 million. You don't mind me presuming that you have a million, do you?" (He didn't).

It was then explained to Mr. Geldt that if he really happened to be a millionaire he certainly wouldn't be keeping his money in a bank. He would hire professional investment managers who would select numerous investment propositions and spread the money out amongst them.

"Now then, Mr. Geldt," the salesman would say, "unless you have been keeping something from me you don't have a million." However, the benefits of millionairehood could be available to even the smallest of investors. You too could have the advantages, Mr. Geldt would be told, "of a millionaire's method of investing." This was a mutual fund.

Computations were then produced, suggesting that a mutual fund investor could expect to see $10,000 turn into $54,000 within 10 years. "If this happened to you, Mr. Geldt, would you have been pleased?" the salesman would ask. And it was not even necessary to have $10,000 to put up at once. Just $100 a month for 10 years would result in a pay-out of $34,000.

Cornfeld, clearly, was a man who understood greed and how to exploit it. One beneficial effect of his rise and spectacular fall is that the industry has since been more tightly controlled. The Financial Services Act of 1986 has had a significant impact on the way in which investment products are sold. There are many respectable funds, on both sides of the Atlantic, which have performed well. But there will always be an element of risk.

Some advisers specialize in particular fields. They claim to be experts in commodities or financial futures. Perhaps they are, but small investors would do well to stay clear of them.

Putting money into commodities is, as someone once said, "like climbing aboard a big dipper which has no brakes and no seat belts." The people who are drawn to this kind of speculation are not investors but gamblers. They want *action* — the sort of mercurial price movements that can mean big profits in a relatively short period of time. They rarely take delivery. In 95 deals out of 100 the whole affair is strictly a paperchase. If you have made the wrong guess, losses can mount rapidly. It takes strong nerves and a deep pocket to stay in the game.

The same goes for financial futures that were born amid the soy beans and pork bellies of the hectic Chicago commodity exchanges in the early 1970s. They come in two basic forms: interest rates and foreign currency. An interest rate future consists of a contract to buy or sell a given amount of a particular type of fixed income security (bonds, Treasury bills, even mortgages) for an agreed price at some future date. The value of the securities covered by the contract is struck and a delivery date is set, which could be a year or more, though one to six months is more common. If rates go up the value goes down, and vice versa. A speculator who expects a decline in rates buys into the market, gambling that the value of his contract will rise above the agreed price by the time he has to pay the full amount.

A currency future is, quite simply, a contract to buy or sell a given amount of a specific currency, such as the dollar or sterling, for an agreed price at a future date. In other words, the principle is the same. With currencies so much more volatile than they used to be, this may seem like an appealing proposition. But it is primarily a market for professionals, such as fund managers and company treasurers who want to "hedge" against currency movements. It isn't worth dabbling in currency futures if one only has a few thousand dollars available.

How Good are Bonds?

The safest investments are widely believed to be government bonds. The label has a comforting ring: governments can't go broke, can they?

Perhaps not. But they can be overthrown, which is what happened in Russia and China. When the communists gained power, they refused to honor the bonds issued by their predecessors. Numerous people who had invested their money in them lost everything. The impressive-looking pieces of paper became known as "lampshade bonds" because the only consolation for the poor investors who were stuck with them was that they made nice lampshades.

Governments can also run into such serious debt problems that they find it difficult to meet their obligations — or they choose not to do so. Countries in Latin America used to be notorious for this, and there are still regimes which cannot be trusted to keep their word. It affects their credit rating, of course, but political considerations may be paramount. In short, the popular notion that *all* government bonds are safe is a myth.

Countries like Britain and the United States are in a different league. They honor their commitments regardless of who may be in power. We may change leaders, but no Chancellor of the Exchequer or Secretary of the Treasury would ever dream of defaulting. The consequence for the whole system of public financing would be horrendous.

Interest is paid with unfailing regularity and fixed repayment dates are invariably honored. But it doesn't mean that you won't lose money.

In Britain, government bonds are known as "gilt-edged securities," which implies that they are as good as cash in the bank. It is, alas, another myth. Some of the best-known gilts have been a great disappointment. A good example is War Loan 3.5 percent, which was sold in £100 units during the First World War. People were told that they would be redeemed in 1952 "or after." Those two words "or after" have turned out to be one of the most crafty tricks ever played on British investors. It means, or seems to mean, eternity.

Because there is no specific commitment to repay, many factors can influence the market value of these gilts — the general level of interest rates, the state of sterling, the rate of inflation, and so on. Dated stocks are a much better bet, but they are subject to the same kind of influences. If you don't want to take the risks associated with shares, they are worth a closer look. But don't fall for the argument that you cannot go wrong — and don't expect them to beat inflation.

There are also bonds issued by towns and cities, and by large corporations. Many local governments have a good track record, but prices can go down as well as up. The best thing that can be said about the fixed interest securities of companies is that they have a higher claim on the assets than holders of ordinary shares. But that may be of little use if the companies go bust.

Golden Illusions

An even greater myth is that one can always rely on gold.

The yellow metal still has a strong hold on the imagination. It is widely regarded as the ultimate investment, the one currency which will never fail you. The late General de Gaulle (who seemed obsessed by the stuff) summed it up long ago. "There can be no other criterion, no other standard than gold," he declared. "Yes, gold, which never changes, which can be shaped into ingots, bars and coins, which has no nationality and which is considered in all places and at all times at the fiduciary issue par excellence."

In all places and all times? If you walked into your local supermarket tomorrow and put down a gold bar or Krugerand at the check out counter, you would be regarded as a crank. I feel more inclined to agree with Keynes, who called it "a barbarous relic."

Croesus, King of Lydia (Western Turkey), introduced the first gold coins in 550 B.C. and, in the many centuries that followed, gold was widely used in trade. But it was not until 1867 that the European states got together in Paris and agreed that it would henceforth be the reserve against deposits and note circulation and the means of payment between countries.

As long as the metal was being paid to the people who came for it, a country was on the gold standard. If you had gone to the Bank of England in the 1920s, and presented a £5 note for payment in gold, the promise would be honored. The arrangement was suspended during the First World War but remained in place until 1931, when the gold standard was abolished. Today the Bank of England would simply give you a crisp new £5 note.

In the United States, President Roosevelt passed a law in 1933 which forbade Americans to hold gold. But the monetary link was maintained until 1971, when President Nixon was forced to cut it. The law was subsequently repealed.

In that decade, the South African mining companies hit on an idea which would bring gold within the reach of people who could not possibly afford a gold bar. They devised the Krugerand — a coin which contained exactly one troy ounce of pure gold. It was legal tender, its value could easily be determined at any time by reference to the gold price, and it could be bought and sold through dealers all over the world. The

Krugerand swiftly acquired an enthusiastic following and other countries, including Canada and Mexico, also got into the act.

Millions of investors agreed with de Gaulle's argument. Gold seemed to
offer the best protection against devaluation, political upheavals, and
war. Paper money might become worthless; property could be confis-
cated; companies in which one had invested one's savings could go
under. Gold would always find a buyer. That, at least, is what they firmly believed — and if enough people believe in something it has its own
momentum.

By the beginning of the 1980s, the metal had reached an all-time peak
of $850 an ounce and people were lining up at London's Hatton Garden
to sell unwanted gifts and family heirlooms for cash, so that dealers
could melt them down. But the market cracked, and when it did there
was a scramble to get out of gold. People rushed to take profits while
they could still do so. It has never recaptured its former glory. Since that
crazy boom, it has underperformed the *Financial Times* All-Share index
by more than 80 percent. By early 1997, the price was down to around
$350 an ounce.

No one knows, at any given time, how much might come on to the market. It is this factor, more than anything else, that has made gold such a
lousy investment. There are 35,000 tons stashed away in the vaults of
central banks, gathering dust. It is hard to believe that any of them is
interested in buying more; it is much more likely that some of it will be
sold. Private hoarders are sitting on a lot of the stuff, waiting for a new
boom that may never come. Mining companies in various parts of the
world are still busy adding to the stock.

It seems absurd that, in a sophisticated age, so much time and effort
should be expended on digging stuff out of one hole and burying it in
another, thousands of miles away. Not surprisingly, many economists
agree with Keynes rather than de Gaulle.

Gold earns no interest for the investor and has to be protected. Whether
or not one should buy it depends largely on what you think will happen
to the world in the years ahead. If you believe in some of the fashionable

doomsday scenarios, you may feel better with a few piles of coins under your mattress. If not, you will fare better with equities.

John Maynard Keynes once made what still strikes me as valid comment on the subject of performance. He wrote:

> The social object of skilled investment should be to defeat the dark forces of time and ignorance which envelop our future. The actual, private object of the most skilled investment today is to "beat the gun," as the Americans so well express it, to outwit the crowd, to pass the bad, or depreciating half-crown to the other fellow.

> This battle of wits to anticipate the basis of conventional valuation a few months hence does not even require the gulls amongst the public to feed the maws of the professional; it can be played by the professionals amongst themselves. Nor is it necessary that anyone should keep his simple faith in the conventional basis of valuation having any genuine long-term validity. For it is, so speak, a game of Snap or Old Maid, or Musical Chairs — a pastime in which he is victor who says Snap neither too soon or too late, who passes the Old Maid to his neighbor before the game is over, who secures a chair for himself when the music stops. The game can be played with zest and enjoyment, though all the players know that it is the Old Maid which is circulating, or that when the music stops some of the players will find themselves unseated.

Today, stock markets are widely regarded as little more than casinos. The professionals naturally resent this. They prefer to portray them as vital parts of economies, "oiling the wheels of industry" and providing people with the opportunity to make profitable use of their savings. But Keynes was right: it is a game. The players don't want to get involved in the management of companies they invest in, and they don't much care what happens to a company when it is taken over; it is enough that they have placed their chips on a lucky number. Many consider the small investor to be a bit of a nuisance. They can make more money by dealing with financial institutions or trading on their own account. The players reckon they have the edge. But, as we have seen, there are times when the game gets out of hand. One of the oldest firms in London, Barings, was bought down by a young man who was thought to be a financial genius. His name is Nick Leeson and he is currently sitting in a Singapore jail.

The Myth of the Wicked Gnome

A GOOD DEAL OF PRIVATELY OWNED GOLD IS KEPT IN THE vaults of Swiss banks. There are obvious reasons for this. Switzerland has long been regarded as haven for the rich who are determined to protect their fortunes from the vicissitudes of war, inflation, and confiscation. Neutrality, financial freedom, low taxes, and bank secrecy are an appealing combination. For many people, having gold or other assets in a Swiss bank is not just an investment or a habit — it is the ultimate safeguard against social and fiscal chaos.

Some of the gold (no one knows how much) was deposited by wealthy Jewish facilities when Hitler came to power in the 1930s because they feared, with good cause, that they would be persecuted by the Nazis. Many later perished in the Holocaust and their descendants have fought a vigorous campaign to force the Swiss to hand it back. They have accused them of willfully keeping assets given to them for safekeeping. Switzerland rejected these charges for many years but in early 1997 the government issued a decree setting up a fund for Holocaust victims. It also decided that, in order to get at the facts, the bank secrecy laws would no longer apply to such assets. The president said that it did so "to protect the country's good reputation." The reality is that the Swiss feared a boycott by Jewish business people, particularly Americans.

Throughout the 20th century, the Swiss have had a special place in business folklore — not because of their watches, cheeses, and army knives but because of the many legends associated with their banks. Some undoubtedly contain an element of truth, but most of them are myths.

It was a British Minister, George Brown, who invented the offensive label "Gnomes of Zurich." He blamed them for causing the Labor government of Harold Wilson great difficulties, in the 1960s, by speculating against the pound. Other countries were doing the same, but the Swiss made convenient scapegoats. No one liked them: they were considered to be too smug, too self-centered, too obsessed with money. The public was therefore all too ready to accept the myth that they, not the Ministers, were responsible for the need to introduce painful new economic measures.

Americans have been equally ready to believe the sweeping allegations so often made against Swiss banks. It is widely believed that they shield foreign criminals involved in narcotics, vice, white slavery, fraud, and other rackets. The charges are unjustified. All these things are major crimes in Switzerland and are taken seriously. The country is a charter member of Interpol and the banks are quite willing to cooperate if it can be shown that the depositor has been engaged in criminal activities. Swiss banking is not orthodox by American or British standards, but the vast majority of banks are both legitimate and rather staid. None will knowingly act as a clearing house for the Mafia or any other criminal organization.

Yet the myth persists, partly because it has been perpetuated by Hollywood movies and lurid novels, but also because there is still disagreement about the definition of crime. The Swiss do not feel obliged to enforce the laws of other nations — or, for the matter, to make moral judgments. Whether bank secrecy will be invoked or not comes down to what is considered a crime in Swiss courts. Many countries, including the United States and Britain, have strict rules against tax evasion but it is not a crime in Switzerland. (Tax fraud is, but they define it very narrowly and will only take action in the most blatant cases.) The same applies to exchange controls and dealings in gold.

Another reason why the myth continues to have such a strong hold is, of course, that secrecy makes it all too easy to indulge in rumors and guesswork. The press frequently prints stories about Swiss banks which they cannot deny without revealing the facts, which would in most cases break their own laws.

A key element in this secrecy is the famous numbered account. As the label indicates, a client is known by a number instead of a name. Only two or three officers of the bank know a patron's true identity. The system greatly reduces the chances of either being bribed or accidental betrayal of a foreign customer by a bank employee. It is often said to have been invented to help criminals, but that has never been its purpose. Banking secrecy (and the numbered account) only became part of Swiss law in 1934 to prevent Nazi agents from tracking down the assets of German citizens — many of whom were later able to retrieve them. It is still kept as a means of giving a client more privacy, but the Swiss are adamant that it does not protect anyone involved in activities which their courts regard as a crime. Anyone who thinks that it is possible to walk in off the street with a suitcase full of cash and open a numbered account is badly mistaken. Banks insist on a reference or an introduction by someone they know.

Many people have discovered, to their cost, that it is dangerous to trust the myths. American author Clifford Irving wrote a phony autobiography of Howard Hughes and attempted to put the proceeds into a Swiss bank. They denounced him to the authorities and he was sent to jail for fraud. More recently, a leading member of the Moscow Mafia was arrested in Geneva and held on a charge of money laundering and membership of a criminal organization. Other Russians have been charged with trafficking in false passports, control of prostitution rings, and operating protection rackets.

Like many other foreigners, the Russians have also learned something else about the Swiss; they don't encourage immigration. The country already has a high proportion of foreign residents — 19 percent — and permits have become extremely hard to get.

Switzerland manages more than one-third of cross-border private banking assets around the world. The center of this is not Zurich but Geneva, which has 160 banks as well as hundreds of investment managers. They are obviously good at it, but the popular idea that Swiss bankers are better than everyone else is another myth. They are among the first to concede that there is just as much expertise in London or New York.

Other Tax Havens

They also recognize that companies and individuals nowadays have a much wider choice of tax havens than in the past. There are said to be more than 50 around the world, though many prefer to call themselves "offshore financial centers" because it sounds more dignified. Most of them are small countries with very little in the way of natural resources and wealth. Modern methods of communications ensure that they can stay in touch with their clients. The concept of numbered accounts has been widely copied, and some tax havens have adopted tighter secrecy laws than the Swiss. They are perfectly aware that many of the foreigners are engaged in activities which their own governments have declared illegal, but like the Swiss they don't consider themselves to be bound to enforce other people's laws. If a country has no income tax it cannot be a crime to evade it.

The tiny state of Liechtenstein is considered to be one of the most secure destinations, and places like the Bahamas and the Channel Islands have also gained ground because of tax advantages. All say that they will not aid criminals but the Swiss say that some of their rivals are more accommodating than they are. One certainly has to wonder how billions of dollars are laundered every year. Little of the cash actually stays there: once it has passed through, it is moved abroad and invested in stocks, real estate, and legitimate enterprises. The growing use of electronic money transfers has raised problems over jurisdiction and the speed of transactions and volumes involved have made monitoring difficult. In many cases it is hard to trace the origin of funds and harder still to get a conviction.

Investigators from America and Britain have been known to resort to all kinds of tricks in their constant battle to discover the identity of people who use tax havens. They have, for example, bribed bank employees and auditors. The IRS once mounted an operation which rivaled the exploits of the CIA or *Mission Impossible* for ingenuity. One caper involved an attractive female informer who, while visiting the manager of a bank in the Bahamas, slipped a Rolodex containing names, addresses and telephone numbers into her handbag. She also entertained the manager while he was in Miami on business. During the evening out, government agents entered his hotel room and photographed the contents of his briefcase, which included information on a man the IRS was investigating.

Another hazard, seldom acknowledged, is that the people who have your money may use it to finance ventures which end in disaster. The wilder offshore fringes include funds dabbling in all manner of derivatives, or which invest directly in commodities and property and gear up by borrowing heavily against their underlying assets. Looser regulations in places such as the Caribbean have spawned large hedge funds with few investment constraints.

A foreigner who believes that he has been fleeced by an unscrupulous operator may find little justice in the local courts. Indeed, by attracting attention to himself he may end up a double loser; if he is a tax evader the Revenue agents of his own country will be after him like a shot.

There are other possible pitfalls, especially in the less stable countries. Laws may be changed suddenly or the person using the facilities may lose everything in a political upheaval.

Many people dream of retiring to a tax haven in the sun — Monaco, perhaps, or on one of those palm-fringed islands. They imagine that, freed from the burden of taxes, they can make their income go a long way. But that may turn out to be another myth. The more secure havens are often very expensive places to live in and much of the gain from tax avoidance may be swallowed up by a considerable increase in the cost of living.

T·W·E·N·T·Y-O·N·E

The Myth about Inflation

ONE OF THE MAIN REASONS THAT GOLD WAS SO WIDELY touted in the 1970s was fear of runaway inflation. These were the years when the inflation rate in many countries hit record levels. It never happened and, as we have seen, gold turned out to be not such a good bet after all. But it is easy to understand why inflation frightened so many people — and still does.

There is a story about a man who decided to have himself frozen until, at some future date, scientists found a cure for his ailment. Before he did so, he called his stockbroker and asked to put all his money into future growth situations. Time passed, a cure was found, and his guardians had him defrosted. One of his first acts was to call the broker's office. "Tell me," he said, "how have my stocks done over the past 60 years?"

"Oh yes," said the voice at the other end, "my grandfather told me about you. One moment, while I check . . . . Well, they have had their ups and downs, you know, booms, slumps, war and peace, but your account is now worth over $6 million."

"That's marvelous," he said. "No more money worries — I can really enjoy living again." At this point the operator cut in, "That will be $60,000 for the next three minutes, please."

For anyone who experienced Germany's hyper-inflation of the 1920s, that is a decidedly sick joke. They know what it's like to be broke with lots of money in your pockets. Prices rose by 14,000 percent in a single year. The German mark, which was valued at 4.2 to the dollar in 1921, sank to 11 trillion marks to the dollar in 1924. People carried bank notes in wheelbarrows.

The currency collapsed again after the second world war. I was in Germany at the time, as a young boy, and I have vivid memories of those days. Money became so worthless that it was replaced by barter. Chocolate bars, packets of cigarettes, and tins of coffee were the generally accepted means of exchange. They passed from hand to hand, just as paper currency had done before.

The government decided to take drastic action. The old currency was simply abandoned and on 20 June 1958 everyone in the country was given 40 new marks. The slate was wiped clean and every German made a new start in life with the equivalent of about $15. Since then the authorities have done their utmost to ensure that inflation does not get out of hand again.

More recently, countries in Latin America have struggled with annual inflation of more than 1,000 percent. Britain and the United States have never had to go through anything like that, but the 1970s were bad enough.

Inflation is a process of continually rising prices implying a continually falling value of money. It creates an illusion of wealth, which is why so many people tend to underrate its damaging effects. Earnings, profits and assets all go up. It makes people feel that they are better off — even when they aren't.

Inflation helps to explain why America has more millionaires than ever before. Some have reached that enviable status without any apparent effort: the house they bought years ago could now be sold for a million on the market. But a million is not what it used to be, because everything costs so much more. Inflation is a great deceiver. In management it gives a false impression of two main yardsticks — growth and profit. If the value of money has fallen by half, a company that has doubled its sales and profits has shown no real increase.

The people who are most keenly aware of this are pensioners who saved money for what they believed would be a comfortable old age. They find that it doesn't go as far they thought it would. It is like looking at one's lifetime savings through the wrong end of a telescope. Inflation takes from the old, the weak, the unorganized and the poor, and gives to those who are strongly in control of their own income.

I once saw a bumper sticker that said, "inflation is a stab in the buck" and graffiti which declared, "I'm 300 percent against inflation." I also like this comment I saw in an American magazine, "There's one consolation. The money you don't have isn't worth what it once was." Not very sophisticated, I grant you, but close enough to the truth.

Beating Inflation

In recent years, many governments have fought a largely successful battle against inflation. There is, today, a better understanding of its causes and dangers, and we have more sophisticated techniques for controlling key factors like the money supply. New myths have emerged in the process. One is that high interest rates (one of the main weapons) are a good thing because they give savers a larger income. But they merely compensate them to some extent for the fall in the value of their money. The downside is that they also make it more expensive to borrow, which hits home buyers and small companies. Another myth is that a high level of unemployment is needed to ensure low inflation. In fact, there is no reliable way of measuring the relationship. In past years we have had both high unemployment and rapid inflation.

Despite this success, many people fear that we shall see more trouble in future and are casting around for protection. If gold won't do it, what about diamonds? They have long enjoyed the same kind of glamorous reputation, and there are many parts of the world where they remain very popular. Diamonds are easy to transport, easy to conceal, and an international asset. They have helped countless refugees to move their wealth from one country to another, and they have proved to be a handy little nest-egg for young women at the end of a hectic romance. But the notion that diamonds are a reliable investment is another myth. The industry is notoriously volatile.

When inflation was running at high levels, people were also persuaded to put their money into all kinds of other investments which were said to have an excellent chance of holding their value — paintings, silver, antique furniture, ceramics and even stamps and Victorian bric-a-brac. Almost any asset was a candidate simply because it was a physical thing rather than a piece of paper. "You can't lose money in art" became a popular slogan. Dealers developed a nice line in sales talk, with lots of references to inflation and currency upheavals.

But, as many people have discovered to their cost, it tends to be a lot easier to buy than to sell it. One of the most popular TV series in the UK has been the *Antiques Roadshow*. People are often amazed at the values quoted by experts, but you seldom hear whether they have actually been able to get those prices. Many of the paintings that were appreciating so rapidly a decade ago on a wave of speculative buying — 18th century watercolors and so on — have turned out to be poor investments.

The big salesrooms, especially Sotheby's and Christie's, are protected from national recessions by their global operations. There is always an economy booming somewhere, and usually enough of the newly enriched locals spend some of their fortunes on the national art. The mega-rich also remain addicted to Van Goghs and Picassos. But it is nonsense to apply this to all works of art, let alone Aunt Bertha's silver teapot.

I take a rather old-fashioned view of the whole business. I have some good paintings, and several fine pieces of antique furniture, but I didn't look upon them as investments and I don't now. I am too attached to them to ever think of selling.

I was appalled when pension funds and financial institutions moved into the market. They stashed away paintings which no one ever saw. It's hardly the fate their creators envisaged, and it struck me as a dreadful waste. I am still put off by people who insist on telling everyone what their collection is worth. I once went to a dinner party given by a wealthy property owner who owned some works by L. S. Lowry. A fellow guest, one of the richest men in Britain, had never heard of Lowry before and didn't like his paintings. They reminded him too much of his northern origins. But he showed greater interest when our host told him how much their value had risen. Indeed, he talked of nothing else for the rest of the evening and he later became the owner of several Lowrys himself. He still doesn't like them, but he thinks they are a good investment.

The same kind of attitude has, alas, invaded other fields. During my years as editor of *Punch* I had numerous letters from people who owned bound volumes of the magazine and wanted to know if they had value. They were not referring to the contents. Value meant money. I grant you that volumes of *Punch* do not necessarily constitute art (though some of the cartoons certainly qualify) but I think you will understand why I wrote rather scathing replies.

There are tales galore of stupendous gains made by skillful investors in art, but there have also been some spectacular misses. There is absolutely no guarantee that you will see a profit even if you buy acknowledged works of famous people. No one ever really knows what art is worth, in money terms, until it is sold. In 1995, average sales prices at Christie's auctions in Britain and America were less than half of their 1990 levels.

A common fallacy is that all the real assets people might want to hold were produced in the past. It leads to the assumption that, since the supply is fixed, growing demand is sure to boost their value. But collectors also go for works by new painters, sculptors, silversmiths and other artists. Who knows what they will want to buy in future? There are dealers who will tell you that, if you want a hedge against inflation, you should go for pop memorabilia, film posters, classic cars, and teddy bears. They may be right, but they may also turn out to be horribly wrong.

A point seldom made about inflation is that the figure one sees quoted in the news and the one which matters to the individual are quite separate concepts. As noted earlier, the official rate is based on a retail price index which covers a wide range of products and services. But we all have our own rate of inflation, depending on our lifestyles. Individual spending habits do not replicate the index. Pensioners, for example, tend to spend a larger proportion of their income on food and fuel than younger people. So the question should really be: what do you think you will need in order to maintain the lifestyle you want? The tricky part, obviously, is to anticipate what will happen to the cost of most important items and history suggests that it pays to err on the side of pessimism.

People with index-linked pensions are in a better position than others. Some forms of savings are also linked to the index. But this may not be enough, which is why many of us have also invested in shares.

I firmly believe that the best investment one can make is still one's home. It is solid; paper currencies may come and go but a good house or apartment will be there for a long time to come. It is, moreover, an investment one can use. But there is no automatic correlation between inflation rates and property values. The idea that "you can't lose money if you buy property" is as much of a myth as the notion that "you can't lose money buying art." Ask all the people who bought homes in the 1980s and then saw an alarming drop in prices. As with all investment, it is very much a matter of making the right choice and buying at the right time.

A key factor is location. Today's fashionable areas can so easily become tomorrow's slums — and vice versa. The people who have saved themselves both money and aggravation are those who have had the good sense not only to spot the decline in the areas in which they are living, which isn't difficult, but also to sell while others are still willing to move into them.

London has greatly benefited from its role as an international business center. The market has been sustained by foreign buyers, who reckon that Britain is likely to enjoy greater political stability in the 21st century than their own countries. Here again, though, it would be foolish to assume that the supply is fixed. Rising value prices are a powerful incentive for developers.

What about a second home? In theory, a country cottage or a place in the sun should be an asset you can enjoy and which can always be sold if the going gets rough. But the same rules apply.

The sun makes some people extraordinarily gullible. They make down payments on houses and flats which may never be built. They buy tiny studios in ramshackle buildings, in towns and villages they don't really know. They are careless about checking whether the seller has a clear and marketable title. They buy derelict houses in the middle of nowhere, spend their savings on doing them up, and then discover how miserable the place can be in winter. They forget to ask about local taxes and services, or to establish whether or not there are plans to run a highway through the garden. They don't take account of possible currency swings (which can make a big difference to values) or of likely trends in inflation. They don't even ask themselves whether they would be happy if, one day, they lived there all the year round. Reality is suspended.

I have a house in the sun myself — on a small island in the Bahamas — and I have learned one basic lesson. Don't get seduced by all those palm trees and beaches, and don't buy just because you think that it will be a valuable asset. It *may* turn out to be the best thing you ever did, but it could also become a nightmare.

Another Scenario

All the talk about the inflation is based on the belief that it is here to stay, a fact of life as inevitable as taxes. Most of us have grown used to seeing prices rise year after year. But there is another school of thought which holds that the real danger is a collapse into *deflation*.

Most governments nowadays aim for minimal inflation — a small annual increase. The statistics are debatable, as noted earlier, but this has become official policy. It makes sense, but some economists believe that we are more likely to see *falling* prices, for the first time since the 1930s.

A leading exponent of this unorthodox view is Roger Bootle of the HSBC Group, parent of Midland Bank. He gave his reasons in a fascinating book published in 1996, *The Death of Inflation*. I recommend it to any reader who is prepared to consider an alternative scenario.

Bootle argues that, because of what happened in the 1970s, we have "demonized" inflation to such an extent that we cannot see that "the assumptions we should now be making have fundamentally changed."

He thinks that the "inflationary impulses are fading to be replaced by powerful anti-inflationary forces."

You know how I feel about economic theories, but if he is right we will clearly have to reconsider our attitudes.

In this scenario, interest rates will be low and people will be tempted to borrow more. But it will be harder to secure pay rises and to repay debts. People will not be able to count on an increase in house prices, which will do nothing more than creep up and in many years will fall. Antiques and works of art will cease to be regarded as investments and return to being viewed on their intrinsic merits. Savers and pensioners will be better off than in the past, because they will no longer have the need to protect themselves against inflation. They will benefit from falling prices. Companies will no longer be able to work on a "cost-plus" basis; they will have to adjust their thinking to take account of an entirely different environment. There will be an end to the confusion created by inflation.

Bootle maintains that this is the way things were before the onset of perpetual inflation in the years after the Second World War — and that is the world we are returning to. I am not sure about that, but the argument is clearly not without merit.

It should certainly be given careful consideration by the people who make policy decisions. I find it disturbing that so many don't seem to be sure what they are dealing with. In the summer of 1997, the highly regarded chairman of the Federal Reserve, Alan Greenspan, said that the U.S. monetary authorities face a long, uphill task trying to pin down the precise meaning of inflation at a time of fast-rising asset values and technological change. He went on: "there are enough difficult issues of concept and measurements for politicians and academics to keep us occupied for the next 15 years or more." His candid admission inevitably raises a serious question: if even the Fed feels the need to redefine inflation how can it make the right decisions?

T·W·E·N·T·Y-T·W·O

The Myth about Age

IN MUCH OF THE BUSINESS WORLD, THE EMPHASIS is on youth. This has become so firmly established that all kinds of myths are associated with it. The greatest is that people are "over the hill" at 50.

The young, of course, have a vested interest in perpetuating such nonsense. I did much the same when I was in my twenties. I thought that the fellows who were still hanging on to their jobs in middle age should move over. I was impatient and convinced that I could do better. Today's young people are in just as much of a hurry. The difference is that their arguments are more likely to be accepted than they were then. When companies embark on their periodic bouts of downsizing the older employees tend to be the main victims.

Youth has some undeniable advantages: energy, enthusiasm, ambition. But it is as ridiculous to assume that *all* young men and women possess these qualities, and have more to offer, as it is to make sweeping generalizations about people over 50. As an employer I have learned to my cost that many young people are lazy, incompetent and blatantly disloyal. They do more harm than good and should never be allowed to hold senior positions.

Prejudice against older people at work is universal. But they are not an homogenous group, so age is not much use for predicting how someone will perform in a job. "Older" can mean as young as 40. Indeed, some companies seem to take the view that 40 — not 50 — is the stage at which they should "let people go." It may be justified in jobs which demand physical strength, but it is dumb to think that way about management. Chairmen and CEOs certainly don't feel that such broadbrush rules should be applied to them. Most consider themselves to be perfectly capable of running large organizations in their fifties and sixties. Some remain at the helm in their seventies. Shareholders don't seem to mind as long as they keep delivering good results.

So why the discrimination? One widely-used argument is that it often costs more to employ older workers than younger ones. Pay may be linked to seniority rather than to performance, and some occupational pension schemes require larger contributions. Health insurance can also cost more. But this is not necessarily a good reason. The key issue must surely be whether the executive is still the best man — or woman — for the job. People should not be hired or promoted just because they are younger or cheaper. Able managers should not be forced out only because of age. They may have peaked, but they may also have reached the point where they are about to do their best work.

Many employers have found that older workers are more reliable, conscientious and loyal. They tend to be good at dealing with people and happy to work in teams. Fear of losing their jobs can be an additional motivation for trying harder than the young terriers who are snapping at their heels. Their experience can be invaluable when important decisions have to be made. It does not follow that they all have these useful attributes, but they deserve to be judged as individuals rather than as members of the "older generation." If this does not happen as often as it should it is, to a considerable extent, due to popular misconceptions about the process of aging. Here are some of the lies which are told — and, alas, widely accepted:

- ❖ Thinking slows down significantly as you age.
- ❖ You can't teach an old dog new tricks.
- ❖ Intelligence declines with age.
- ❖ People run out of steam once they are 50.

❖ Older people are less adaptable and slower to grasp new ideas than younger employees.

It is not difficult to challenge these superficial statements, one merely has to look at history. Copernicus was 70 when he published his analysis of planetary movement, which became the foundation stone of modern astronomy. Christopher Wren finished St. Paul's Cathedral at the age of 79. Charles Darwin produced his revolutionary theory, *On the Origin of Species*, at 50, and Wilhem Roentgen was the same age when he discovered x-rays. Louis Pasteur gave the first successful injection against rabies at 62. Numerous artists have produced great works in old age. Picasso went on painting masterpieces until his death at 93. Many statesmen, too, have made a tremendous impact at a point when, if one believes the myths, they should have "run out of steam." Winston Churchill became Britain's wartime Prime Minister at 66. Mahatma Gandhi won independence for India when he was 77. Need I go on?

Well, perhaps. Take business. Everyone has heard of Colonel Sanders and his ubiquitous Kentucky Fried Chicken. But did you know that he started the business *after* retiring from another job? The Colonel was an amateur cook, and fried chicken was his specialty. He used part of his first social security check of $105 to take a stab at marketing his recipe. Eight years later he sold his company, logo and recipe for $4 million and got himself a nice little contract as a promoter and consultant. Had his thinking slowed down when he retired? Had his intelligence declined? Was the old dog no longer able to learn new tricks? Of course not. Umpteen young people can fry chickens, but how many can turn such a basic process into something worth millions?

The Colonel's story is by no means unusual. It is remarkable how many people, all around the world, have launched and developed a business in what is nowadays called The Third Age. It can be heady stuff. The kids have grown up, the pension is assured, and you have money in the bank. Why not have a go at something which you have always wanted to do?

I started a new company when I was 57. My thinking had not slowed down; it had become more tightly focused. I had a clearer idea of what I wanted to do than when I first went into business at 42. I also had a better understanding of the opportunities and pitfalls. The company has prospered.

A famous American baseball player once asked a profound question, "How old would you be if you didn't know how old you were?" The answer, of course, depends on one's state of mind. If you believe that you are still 35 (as I do) it doesn't really matter what the calendar says. If you are 35 but have the mindset of an older person you will behave like one.

There are two other quotations which have had a big influence on me. The renowned American financier, Bernard Baruch, who lived to be 94, once said that, "Old age is always 15 years older than I am." Andrew Maurois went one better, "Growing old is no more than a bad habit which a busy man has no time to form." At 64, I agree with both of those wise and uplifting sentiments.

I readily concede that not all of us want to start a new business or remain in a management job. Many people are quite happy to settle for part-time work. Others take early retirement and devote themselves to a life of leisure. But there is plainly a big difference between such voluntary acts and being pushed out because of one's age, regardless of conditions and qualifications. If people are fit, productive and want to work, age should be no bar.

Changes

One of the most extraordinary features of the 20th century has been the sharp increase in life expectancy, chiefly because of stunning break-throughs in medicine. In 1899, the average in Britain was 45.5 years for a boy and 49 years for a girl. By the year 1999, the figures are expected to be 74.5 and 80 respectively. Scientists tell us that, in future, many more people will live to 100.

Given this trend, we should be reconsidering what we mean by terms like middle age and old. We should also be changing attitudes, instead of playing by rules designed for a different era. Middle age should mean somewhere between 50 and 70.

The idea that 65 should be the official retirement age began with the German Chancellor Otto von Bismarck, who invented the social security system in 1884. When he did so, few people lived that long. All this has changed, but in countries like Britain the benchmark has stayed the same. Indeed, diplomats and civil servants are compelled to retire even earlier, at 60. Many take up appointments in business because they feel, rightly, that they still have a lot to offer. You have had the benefit of a good education; you know how government works, and you have built up a wide range of contacts. It is worth a lot of money to many companies.

We tolerate ageism to a degree that could never be countenanced in the arena of sexism and racism. It is an appalling waste and it cannot go on for much longer. Falling birthrates have led to a very real prospect of a labor shortage in the years to come. The supply of potential young recruits is declining. Older people represent a ready and flexible supply which employers will not be able to ignore. They will have to hold on to existing staff for longer and encourage others, particularly women who have left to bring up a family, to return to the workforce. Retirement ages will have to rise, perhaps to 70. Indeed, I would go further and banish the word "retirement" altogether — it wrongly conjures up negative perceptions. The ideal would be to have no standard age and leave it to individual decisions. People should be free to agree with their employers when to retire according to their personal circumstances.

The shift in the demographic center of gravity from youth to the later years has other significant implications. For many decades the shape and focus of the consumer market has been largely geared to the young. Products and sales campaigns have been designed with them in mind. Older people have been portrayed as has-beens walking hand in hand towards the sunset, or sitting on the porch in rocking chairs, or pruning roses in a suburban garden. Advertising whiz-kids have dismissed them as wrinklies, crinklies, Jubilee Johnnies, and Golden Oldies. But marketing experts now recognize the need for a new approach. There are now more Americans over 50 than ever before. This growing segment of the market is not going to respond favorably to offensive labels and condescending sales messages.

Many pensioners are struggling to make ends meet, but there are also many older people who are asset-rich. They own property and a sizable portfolio of investment which has grown substantially over the years and which provides a good income. They know that they cannot rely on the state to take care of them, and have made adequate provisions, but they want to enjoy the rest of their life and have the means to do so.

In New York, not long ago, I saw a bumper sticker that said, "I am spending my children's inheritance." It made good sense to me. I have never subscribed to the view that parents have an obligation to toil through life so that they can leave as much as possible to their offspring. If the young are going to be pushy and selfish, we can do the same.

There is obvious growth potential in areas like health care, but the scope is much wider. What we eat; what we wear; where, how and when we travel; what we buy for the home; and what we do with our leisure time will all be affected. We don't want to be patronized. We want to be portrayed as active and vital, and we want products and services which will not only make us feel good but also convey that perception to others.

For cosmetic companies this determination to look young promises to be a bonanza on a par with the California gold rush. No one wants wrinkles, and both men and women are eager buyers of products that seem likely to keep them at bay. Fashion designers have always been well aware of the purchasing power of the rich, but are now targeting "seasoned consumers" from all walks of life. So are manufacturers of sports equipment like tennis racquets and golf clubs. Travel companies are expecting substantial growth in the market for cruises and other types of vacations with proven appeal for older people. In Florida and other parts of the United States there are numerous "active lifestyles communities." Some are golfers, sailors, or riding enthusiasts. All offer the opportunity to keep busy and physically fit, and to enjoy the company of like-minded people.

I have nothing against the young. I have children and grandchildren, and I naturally wish them well. They are in many ways the lucky generation. What I resent is the obsession with youth, the bias against older people, the arrogant and foolish view that anyone over 50 is "out of the game" or deserves to be.

The Myth about Gender

THE PREJUDICE IS SAID TO BE EVEN GREATER IF ONE is older and female. There are no doubt companies where this is true, but much has changed in recent years. Women who complain that sex is still discriminated against in business don't exactly miss the point, but they are missing the trend. While politicians and intellectuals talk endlessly about women's rights, ambitious females are making the kind of progress earlier generations could only dream about.

When this century began, almost no suitable careers were open to women whose social class precluded factory work or domestic service. A middle-class woman had little chance of becoming a doctor, an architect, an accountant, or an engineer. The worlds of finance and big business were equally impenetrable. The doors that prevented her from entering either the professions or commerce, on any level higher than shopkeeping, were kept securely bolted by the widely-held belief that women were by nature unfit for most serious occupations. Today there are not only numerous female doctors and architects but also judges, senior police officers, scientists, politicians, newspaper editors, airline pilots, finance directors, bankers, chief executives, and successful entrepreneurs. Women now account for half of all professional, managerial and executive positions.

Despite this, we still hear complaints about the "glass ceiling" — the invisible barrier that is said to keep women from the top. They are based chiefly on the fact that men continue to dominate boardrooms. It is a privilege of dubious value, as noted in an earlier chapter. Membership of a board does not necessarily mean that one has reached "the top." But there is every reason to believe that, in future, many more companies will be run by female CEOs. Studies have shown that the more women there are at a particular managerial level, the more likely it is that other women will be hired or promoted to that level — and the greater the chances that they will get to sit on company boards. The glass ceiling that once appeared to block women's advancement is cracking as they hammer at it from below. *The Economist* reckons that a glass ladder might now be a more appropriate metaphor: women can climb to the top, but the upper rungs are slippery.

This, of course, also applies to men. The idea that, unlike women, we are all treated as equal is a myth. We, too, face tough competition for the best jobs. Men discriminate against each other all the time, often on the grounds of class or race as well as age. Demands for equal status must, therefore, be part of a total battle against prejudice and they must be based on the principle of equal opportunity, not enforced equality.

Women are entitled to protection against blatant sex discrimination. They are not entitled to claim privileges denied to others. Women who go after prestigious jobs should not assume that, if they are turned down, it *must* be because of their sex. It may simply be that they are not considered to be up to the job, or that there are others with better qualifications. The same thing happens to men, who have no choice but to accept it.

Some women maintain that discrimination should work in their favor — that they should be given appointments because there *ought* to be more women in senior positions. This is not liberation, it is deliberate provocation. There is no reason why men should put up with it. One cannot argue that discrimination is evil and then suggest that it is justified because women need to "catch up." Appointments should be made on merit — that, after all, was the crux of the whole women's lib argument.

Happily, this is exactly what appears to be happening. Women are getting there because they have proved themselves to be just as capable —

if not more so — than their male colleagues. Gender has increasingly come to be regarded as irrelevant.

The trend is irreversible. One major reason is the changing nature of work. The growing emphasis on information and services, instead of manufacturing, has led society to place greater value on knowledge than on physical strength. The jobs of people in these growing sectors are not performed on an assembly line and cannot be managed as though they were. They require different skills, which women can acquire as easily as men. They also call for better education. It is significant, in this context, that girls tend to be better at school than boys and that there are more female university graduates than ever before. Many will become the business leaders of the 21st century.

Inevitably there are now attempts to portray men as victims. This nonsense has been encouraged by authors like Jane McLoughlan, who wrote that "one of the anthropological pleasures of the 1990s will be watching how men cope with a new role — that of the redundant male." Others seem to think that, if men are down, they should be given an extra kick. June Stephenson, a feminine psychologist, argues that a special tax should be imposed on males because they are the main perpetrators of crime. The idea is ludicrous. If you go down this road it is just as logical to argue that fat people should be taxed more heavily because they are more prone to heart disease. The fundamental problem with such an approach is that it institutionalizes a divisive blame culture — every group is looking to put the blame on others.

It is decidedly premature to detect the caponized male, redundant at work and at home, under-appreciated anywhere, and driven to crime and loony male-bonding exercises in the woods. I certainly don't feel anxious because "the traditional role of men" has been challenged. On the contrary, I welcome the competition.

An Old Problem . . .

The one remaining barrier has nothing to do with sexism. It consists of a familiar problem: the need to balance the demands of work and family. Many employers are concerned about the practical implications, especially the risk that female executives will put their families before their careers. No one can blame them for doing so, if that is what they want, but it is certainly a factor which has to be taken into account — especially if a company has invested a great deal of money in training women for senior management.

Men are reluctant to admit that it bothers them, but some female writers have acknowledged that this is not an issue which can be brushed aside. "Many single women," one said, "still operate on the basis that their whole lives may change depending on who they marry, or a pregnant woman may reserve the option to turn into an earth mother after her first child, depending on how motherhood takes her." Polly Toynbee has put it another way, "It is not the glass ceiling that holds women back from rising high, it is the children hanging on to their hems."

Various solutions have been proposed — career breaks, job-sharing, part-time work, flexible hours, increased child care facilities, and so on. They may seem fair and sensible, but would they solve the problem? If deals are to be done, or crises managed, the timetable is dictated by events, not by personal considerations. Top executives have to be where they are needed, when they are needed. A line manager who has to meet the next quarter's sales target is not expected to insist on job-sharing or extended maternity leave. Employers want to have a core of long-term, highly committed executives in strategic positions. It is not an unreasonable attitude in today's highly competitive business climate.

Women in well-paid senior management posts are generally able to pay for child care. For many, the biggest problem is not discrimination at work but the fact that their partners do not want them to pursue high-flying careers. They don't want a wife who is just like them — obsessed with office politics, promotion, success. They have no wish to spend their evenings discussing business and they don't go along with the notion that they must shoulder an equal share of parenting and domestic chores. What for? Don't they earn enough for both? What most of them want is a supportive wife, not another rival. There are plenty of attractive women who will gladly settle for that role, which is why so many successful female executives sooner or later find that their marriage is falling apart. It is all terribly unfair, but that is the risk they face.

...And Some Solutions

There is an obvious answer: don't get married, don't have children, be as single-minded as ambitious men. Many career women are doing just that. They refuse to be tied down. Sex is readily available outside marriage and modern methods of birth control make it simple enough to avoid parenthood. A woman may want to marry and have children, but she is not compelled to do so. She has a *choice*.

It is, of course, possible to find a partner who takes a different view — one who actively encourages his wife to climb the ladder and accepts the need to help at home. In years to come an increasing number of couples are likely to reverse roles, with husbands giving up their jobs (or losing them) and deciding to settle for the domestic scene. But it is also likely that many more women will be asking themselves whether they really want to make the sacrifices needed to get to the top. It is already happening.

Penny Hughes, a former president of Coca-Cola in Britain, alienated many of her sisters when she announced that she was giving up her $500,000 a year job to enjoy being with her baby. She has since collected several non-executive directorships, which has given her the flexibility and independence that corporate life cannot provide. Many others have made a similar decision — by no means always because they preferred motherhood. Anne Robinson, the broadcaster and columnist, has given another reason. "Wherever I go these days," she wrote in *The Times*, "I find myself bumping into exhausted female executives. They stand there in their little black suits and you know that the second sentence they are going to utter is the agonized wail 'I am so tired,' followed by a laundry list of the hours they have worked and then the final cry of the New Age corporate woman victim: 'Relationship? You must be joking.'"

Ms. Robinson went on, "If all these weary women were mothers, juggling with babies, nannies, and indolent partners, they might have an excuse of sorts. But they are not. They are sensitive, intelligent souls grimly hanging onto the career ladder while privately being wiped out by the sheer nastiness of it all."

Baroness Howe, chairman of Opportunity 2000, says that "many women are moving away from conventional corporate life. They are devising their own work patterns and their own workplaces by running their own companies." It is a valid point, overshadowed by all that talk of glass ceilings. More than 800,000 women in Britain now run their own business. In America, too, they are setting up shop at an awesome pace. Since 1987 the number of woman-owned firms has increased by 78 percent to eight million. This is another trend which is sure to continue, though one should not underrate the hard work required to succeed. It may sound like poor compensation for failing to become CEO of a big corporation, but it has undeniable attractions — including the enticing prospect of making a fortune.

Not surprisingly, many of these companies provide products and services which appeal to the rapidly growing female workforce. The demographic shift in favor of the older generation has been accompanied by an equally strong increase in the purchasing power of women. This, too, is having a significant impact on the pattern of consumer spending. Women are increasingly courted by designers of homes and makers of cars. The purveyors of popular culture, from books to movies and prime-time television shows, are struggling to cater for what they think are feminine tastes. Women who run their own businesses reckon they have a head start and they are probably right in that assumption. "Women," says a spokesman for the NatWest Bank, "are the business opportunists of the '90s. They are seeing, and even predicting, the gaps in the market and are more ready than ever to chase up the chances provided by the changing world of work." Many male-dominated corporations have been slower to recognize the need for a new approach. The lesson is plain: put more women into senior management positions.

T·W·E·N·T·Y-F·O·U·R

The Bottom Line

IT HAS BEEN SAID THAT IF THERE WERE NO ECONOMIC myths it would be necessary to invent some. The need to maintain public faith in the financial system is often cited in support of this argument. It obviously has some value, but as this book has shown, I believe that most myths do more harm than good. They perpetuate ideas which are false, or out of date, or self-serving, and often lead companies as well as individuals up the garden path.

I do not for one moment expect you to agree with everything that I have said. It would be presumptuous to lay any sort of claim to special wisdom. You may even feel that, in my attempt to demolish myths, I have created some of my own. It is a risk I have been willing to take.

Others may feel that I have not gone far enough. They also have a case. All of us have, at some time or another, come across ideas and suppositions which we have clearly recognized as myths. Many are based on folklore and superstition. Some may be about whole countries. For years it was fashionable to talk about the "economic miracle" in Germany and Japan. But there never was a miracle; they just showed a greater determination to rebuild what was lost in the second world war. They worked harder and more efficiently than people in countries like Britain. In the 1960s it also became fashionable to portray Americans as supermen who would take over Europe. A respected French author, J.J. Servan-Schreiber, called on his countrymen (and other European governments) to erect formidable barriers against the "invasion." Fortunately, they showed more sense. The Americans made numerous investments, but there was no invasion and they did not turn out to be greatly superior to their European colleagues, who proved that point by acquiring a large number of companies in the U.S. and doing a better job than their previous owners. Americans have since created a new myth — that foreigners, particularly the Japanese, are taking over their country. The truth is that they own only a modest percentage of U.S. industry.

As the 20th century draws near, it is fashionable to predict that countries like China will come to dominate world business. I have tried to show that these fears are exaggerated. They take no account of trade and financial barriers, or of the competitive strength of the West in many fields, such as technology and services. They also ignore the fact that many Asian countries have formidable domestic problems — economic, political, social. In China, particularly, these are likely to have priority for quite some time to come. Meanwhile, we would do better to focus on the many opportunities still available in the markets of Asia than to indulge in alarmist speculation about the potential threats. We should certainly not allow ourselves to be taken in by theories and forecasts masquerading as facts.

As we have seen, countless vested interests have strong reasons for preserving popular myths. Economists, management theorists, bankers, lawyers, doctors, investment advisers, consultants and many others benefit from the widely-held belief that they have all the answers. Trade unions maintain that labor is being exploited by wicked capitalists; businessmen say that we would be better off if we had unrestrained economic freedom. Pressure groups use numbers and other alleged "facts" to support strident demands for government intervention. All claim to be acting in "the public interest."

Politicians and media people also like us to believe that their only concern is with the public good. One of their most irritating habits is to tell us what the American people think or want. In reality, they are only expressing a personal view. Market researchers and the "experts" who conduct opinion polls are equally adamant that they know all about our needs and desires, even though there is ample evidence that they frequently jump to the wrong conclusions.

Some businessmen invent stories about themselves or their companies. Press interviews, autobiographies and company histories are often blatant exercises in self-justification or aggrandizement. Some are found out; many are not. The business world needs heroes — they are the role models for the next generation of ambitious young men and women. Even Robert Maxwell was once regarded as a superman. How many more will eventually be seen to have feet of clay?

Showbiz also has a powerful incentive to nurture myths. Not content with spinning tales about Camelot and Robin Hood, it seeks to persuade us that there are alien worlds populated by weird-looking but highly developed beings who plan to invade us, and that there are mysterious creatures like the Yeti and the Loch Ness monster who will one day be "discovered." It is all as absurd as the ancient Greek belief in an assortment of Gods sitting on Mount Olympus, making endless mischief. I find it amazing that so many people still fall for such hokum. It does not seem to matter in the least that we have been to the moon, and even to Mars, and have found no sign of intelligent life. Nor does it count, apparently, that Loch Ness has been thoroughly searched and that the monster has proved to be as elusive as ET.

One can, of course, dismiss these shenanigans as harmless escapists fantasy. But this is plainly not the view taken by the many groups that still insist that the U.S. government is withholding vital evidence that proves the existence of aliens from other planets, or by the scientists who manage to secure substantial grants for their "research." They point out that fiction has often turned into reality. In earlier centuries, there were mythological creatures who could fly to the moon. It was considered to be fanciful, but in the 1960s men did just that. Science is a great destroyer of myths, but it is also capable of making at least some of them come true. Who knows what may happen in the 21st century?

You may well feel that it is a fair question. I have no doubt that the next century will bring more surprises — some pleasant, some not. But it does not mean that we have to accept everything we are told. The truth is that, like the guru game, myths are a lucrative source of revenue and therefore tend to be perpetuated regardless of the facts.

I said at the beginning of this book that I am an incurable optimist. It is an attribute that has served me well for more than half a century. We are all influenced by the views of other people, but ultimately much depends on the individual's attitude and actions. I see no reason why we should allow ourselves to be misled by the great myths of business.

Index

"angels," 111–113
banks, 108–111
companies, 114–115
"vultures," 115

W

wages
  employment and, 4
  equality of, 4
  prices and, 4–5
Waterhouse, Keith, 113
Wellington, Duke of, 46
White, Lord, 91
Wilson, Harold, 30, 41–42
World Bank, 34